HOW TO:

BECOME AN EMAIL NINJA

SEVEN STEPS TO GETTING MORE DONE FASTER IN EMAIL

BY RALPH T. SOULE

Acknowledgements

Books don't write themselves (I wish) and this one would never have seen the light of day without lots of help. I am grateful to my parents, Joan and Lyle Soule, for bringing me into this world, for raising me, and for their plentiful vocabularies, which allowed me to claim to my first-grade phonics teacher that I had never seen a word I didn't know how to pronounce (that changed quickly!). I thank my father for giving me my first thesaurus, opening the wide world of words to me. I learned more things than I can tell from my Grandmother Mary, the smartest person I knew while I was growing up. I hope she would be pleased to learn that I did not burn out before my twenties as she always feared. Thanks to Dr. Ellen Goldman who really taught me to lead the reader and transformed the way I write. Thanks to Neil Yeager, an accomplished author and executive coach whose sage advice and feedback have been so helpful to me for many years. Thanks to Scott Barry who read the draft and provided such useful feedback.

Thanks ever so much to my dear wife Pamela, for the daily encouragement, soft-boiled eggs, unlimited cups of tea, and frequent massages that revived me and kept me going through this journey.

Part 0 - Introduction

That was an amazing email
you sent.

Yup, I have Email
Ninja skills.

Chapter 1-Why this Book?

Bottom Line Up Front (BLUF): This chapter is about why you should care about writing better emails, presents an overview of the book's main ideas, and previews how your thinking about communicating will be transformed as you embark on your Email Ninja journey. This book describes practices, strategies, and tools for using email to get what you want faster and more consistently. The ideas are packaged in a system using the acronym PAASTUB to make it easier to remember and use.

Introduction

Scan the book quickly or jump ahead to any chapter. Go ahead, I'll wait. ... Now that you're back, you probably noticed that this isn't like most other books you've read. That's because I designed it just like an Email Ninja designs his or her email. The sooner you grasp the difference between "writing" and "designing" communications, the faster you will understand that communicating with an email is not just about the writing. As you will learn from reading this book, communicating really isn't about you. At the core of communicating well is designing your message for the reader. *You* may know what you want, but it doesn't matter if you don't convey that well to the reader.

Each chapter of this book begins with a very short bottom line that conveys what the chapter is about, followed by an introduction to the key ideas, and finishes with a summary of those ideas after presenting them in detail. With this design, readers can quickly determine what's important to them and where they want to focus to dramatically improve their ability to communicate in email. I encourage readers to skim the table of contents to see if this book will be of value to them.

This book is a step-by-step guide to getting more done with email than you ever thought possible. Taken individually, the practices, tools, and strategies will probably seem like common sense. Sure, but when has "common sense" ever been common? Combined, the system of this book works like Ninja skills for focusing the reader's attention and overcoming the dark forces of clutter and lack of clarity that plague most emails. Like a Ninja, you can use the skills you learn from this book to achieve amazing, dare I say "startling" results. There, I've said it.

This chapter explains who needs to read this book, why email etiquette is important, the guiding principle at the core of my system, what I mean by Email Ninja, how the book is organized, and how to learn and apply the book's ideas. This book is an off ramp from the to the information superhighway train wreck that email has become. Warning! This book won't *make* you an Email Ninja. It can help you begin your journey to approach email subjects, addressing and composition in entirely new ways. When you finish reading the book, you will think differently about composing, addressing, and "subjecting" email messages to communicate more effectively. Your effort and how you apply your new understanding are entirely up to you.

You should read this book because it will teach you a proven and no-nonsense system for writing better emails right away. If you don't think that would make a huge difference for how you communicate and get things done with email, put the book down and run away now. Before you do, I just have one question. Where are you going to go that communicating more effectively in email or texts won't matter?

What do I mean by "proven, quick, and no-nonsense"? "Proven" means I have honed the practices in this book through years of experience and feedback in real work situations where outcomes matter a lot: the military. These practices are a result of the understandings I developed about effective communications as a Naval Officer and ultimately perfected while I was a Commanding Officer of a large command overseeing the construction of the Navy's latest submarines and aircraft carriers. I have been teaching people to write better emails for decades. They regularly tell me "Wow, I never thought about that" and "Omigosh, those are great ideas."

"Quick" means that I organized this book around checklists and short lists of things that are easy to understand, absorb, and use right away. Quick doesn't mean "easy" to do. Just like becoming a Ninja, you will have to practice to communicate well. It does get easier to do so over time.

"No nonsense" means this book describe my system without fluff or repetition (I ~~hate~~ strongly dislike both). The book stays on point to guide you through a process to produce more effective email messages. Each chapter states the key ideas right away, conveying them briefly and efficiently just like your emails should. This way readers can read the book then get back to work to put the ideas into their practice. The ideas in this book have helped me, helped others, and will help you. Period.

Who Needs to Read This Book

I am not a mind reader, but it is possible that most of the people reading this introduction can be grouped into three main categories. They will be trying to decide whether they should read further.

Category 1 is comprised of people that know they need to read this book. How do they know this?

- They are younger workers that have very little experience sending email. Sometimes called "digital natives," they grew up with ubiquitous Internet connectivity. They send thousands of texts a month, but have trouble understanding why anyone would send a message longer than three sentences.
- These people have never been taught how to compose the text of an email message to make it meaningful and useful to others. Texts don't need subjects so why would emails?
- They send emails that request action and are baffled why it takes so long to get a response, if they get one at all.

Category 2 might be people that desperately need to read this book, but don't realize it. Uh oh, that's a problem. However, the people they work with know they do. They might have even given them a copy of this book. How do their work associates know they desperately need help?

- They send emails with vague, lame subjects like "Tomorrow," "Hello," "October," or "meeting." Let's just be honest: sending an email with a subject like "meeting" is just lame. Don't roll your eyes! These are subjects from emails I receive all the time. These non-descriptive subjects are enormously irritating.
- These people complain about having hundreds of unread emails and not being able to catch up. It takes them days or weeks, if ever, to respond to email that is not from their superiors.

Category 3 is comprised of harried leaders with very little time to read email. These are the people that will skip over emails with subjects like "meeting" while they are scanning their inboxes. They will realize significant life and efficiency improvements by getting the people that send them email to use the practices of this book. What is "inbox" life for people in Category 3?

- They receive hundreds of emails each day, most with vague, opaque subjects from people in category 2.
- They only have time for quick email inbox triage when they can spare a few moments to process email. They need people that send them emails to get the point quickly and be absolutely clear about what action they need.

• They suffer from having to wade through a daily deluge of disorganized and meandering communications from members of their team to find important information.

• They become increasingly irritated after reading the first three paragraphs of an email from their team without being able to understand what it is about.

I make the bold claim that each of these groups will realize significant life and efficiency improvements by following the practices and designing staff email policies based on this book. The remainder of this book backs up this claim.

This book is about getting more done with email than you ever thought possible. My approach to composing and addressing email messages is about focusing on the reader to manage recipient attention like a skilled magician manages his audience's attention to produce results that appear magical (they aren't and most magicians freely admit this). When you finish reading my book, you will think about email subjects and composition in entirely new ways. The book describes a process for composing and addressing email messages based on a tightly integrated system. This means all the parts are important. The book includes tips on email productivity and organization that, combined with skillful message composition, will help you communicate more effectively.

Why I Wrote This Book

My motivation for thinking about better emails was purely selfish. I had several jobs in the Navy where my inbox was filled with poorly written streams of consciousness. I couldn't process it, was constantly behind, and struggled to identify what was important. I spent many hours in the evenings and on weekends, when I should have been with my family, trying to catch up.

Eventually, it dawned on me that I was looking at the problem backwards. Why did I have to do all that work because other people lacked good communication skills? For other performance deficiencies, I helped the people that worked with me overcome them by teaching them how to improve. Why not, I wondered, do the same for email?

I started with an email etiquette guide and revised it over a decade into a set of concrete prescriptions for communicating more effectively. People told me how it helped them. I spent a lot of time thinking about what was wrong and how people could overcome it. I received a lot of feedback on my etiquette guides and did a lot of teaching. My inbox got much clearer, my work-life integration improved, and so did the communications skills of the people I worked with. When I detected backsliding, and there is always backsliding, I guided people back to the better way instead of griped about it. This book is based on the teaching, coaching, and thinking I have done about good and bad email practices over decades.

This book contains very little cognitive science and evolutionary biology about how our brains have not evolved to process emails and text. I am not dismissing the value of science and research. I find cognitive science, biology, and theories about how our brains are more adapted to function in hunter-gatherer societies as stimulating as the next person. Providing there is lots of espresso nearby. I just want to get right to the "good stuff" to make readers as productive as possible as quickly as possible. This book stays on point relentlessly to teach you think about email in completely new ways. I think busy readers will appreciate that as they seek to become much more productive.

Before undertaking a project like this, I wanted to be completely clear about why I was doing it. The reason I wrote this book is that I want to make the world a better place. Really. I think the hardest part of making the world better is deciding where to start. There is a lot you can work on. Some people start by improving access to fresh water.

Others by reducing armed conflict. The best contribution I can make is by reducing the electronic torture people face every day dealing with their email inboxes. I think there is a lot of electronic suffering that can be reduced when people learn to communicate with clear thinking and crisp subjects. This will declutter their minds, significantly improve their email effectiveness, and give them more free time to focus on improving access to fresh water and reducing armed conflict, which are undoubtedly more important in some places than email. I have shared my ideas with many others and every single person has told me that the ideas you are about to learn are dynamite for communicating clearly and effectively.

A few words on what this book is NOT about. While it does include some tips for organizing email and actions, they are not the focus of the book. There are many books and internet resources for that. The book does not propose a simple way to weed out the advertisements, promotions, and just plain creepy stuff in your inbox. There are too many variables involved and the spammers get better all the time at subverting defenses so the strategies have to constantly evolve. This doesn't mean you are on your own against the spammers, just that you won't get much help in your battle against them from reading this book. This book does not provide any instruction on how to write complete sentences and punctuate them properly. There are plenty of books you can read for that.

Call me biased (go ahead, it won't hurt my feelings), but I think everyone that uses email to get things done will benefit from reading this book. It will help them and the people they work with most closely create better messages and become more effective communicators. If that is what you want, read on.

What is etiquette?

The Cambridge Academic Content Dictionary (2016) defines etiquette as "the set of rules or customs that control accepted behavior in particular social groups or social situations." The more general notion of etiquette is that it consists of rules and behavioral conventions that distinguish appropriate behaviors from those considered inappropriate in particular circumstances (Miller, 2002). For something like email, etiquette goes beyond technical matters like how you send and receive messages with some particular application.

Email etiquette encompasses norms and conventions for how you compose, respond to, and address messages.

If the idea of "norms and conventions" with respect to email communications starts to make the hair on the back of your head stand up or your palms sweaty, perhaps it should. Most of us grow up being taught etiquette by our parents or other authority figures for an enormous variety of social situations. This might have included things like how to answer the telephone, interacting with a server in a restaurant, and how to talk to people in authority. We absorb these lessons and internalize them so completely that we seldom think consciously about how to behave most of the time. If we recognize the situation we are in, we have an internal model or script we can access that guides our behavior. Then we just know what to do.

There is almost no similar socializing process for one of the most important business and personal tools of our time: email. Most of the organizational training that I received about email in my career was strictly technical: how to start an email program, open windows, edit and save text, send messages, etc. No one ever spent *a second* teaching me the best way to write a message to get my point across. Instructors must have just assumed that I knew how to write. No one ever told me "Don't email the boss at 3am about your latest project even if you think he is awake," "Don't ramble in email," or "Don't using boring subjects." The fact that people get almost no guidance about how to compose emails has profound implications for the quality of email messages they send.

Many people lack awareness of their poor email practices. Lacking this awareness, they have no motivation for improvement. We often hear about people that commit embarrassing email gaffes that just make you cringe. A colleague profoundly embarrassed by sending something "frank" to the wrong person, talking badly about others in a "confidential" email that is shared widely, or sending salacious details that go viral are frequent occurrences. Few organizations have organizational email etiquette guides a monumental gaffe lessons learned repository. This puts the onus on its members to take responsibility for their own communications practices and learning from the personal lapses or bad examples of others. There's not a lot of learning going on.

That's where this book comes in. This book *is* a systematic approach to improving your email. It has plenty of examples of bad email that will probably remind you of the ineffective things you do. The book is a collection of the best lessons, ideas, practices, and tips that I have seen, developed and taught to change those ineffective practices. The focus of this book is on how to effectively communicate in email and avoid the most likely sources of embarrassment.

Who needs a book on email etiquette? I obviously think we all do, which is the reason I wrote this book. No guide exists like the one you are reading, so hold it carefully. You can find short blog posts and brief articles scattered all over the internet, but not a comprehensive, reinforcing set of rules and behavioral conventions for composing, addressing, subjecting, and replying to email.

What's more, the practices explained in this book form a virtuous cycle for everyone who uses them. Adopting the behaviors will improve your ability to communicate with others. This leads to getting the results that are important to you and your organization more often. Finally, it improves your ability to positively influence the email skills of others. It doesn't get much better than that unless you can find free ice cream.

You cannot control how people think nor how they prioritize their work. It is indeed surprising to me how many people *think* they can. Once you discard that illusion, you *can* start to focus on the practices of this book to make it easier for others to read your email messages, understand what you want, and then give it to you faster. The next section describes the book's layout and how to get the most out of it.

The Book's Guiding Principle

The guiding principle behind the system of email communications in this book is: **focus on the reader**. Peter Drucker put it well, "Before we can communicate, we must know what the recipient expects to see and hear" (Drucker, 1999, p. 393). This requires you to rethink how you approach email composition because "perception has primacy rather than information" (Drucker, 1999, p. 489). Your natural tendency when communicating to others is to focus on yourself: your problem, your needs, and your agenda. This is the wrong approach for getting others to help you.

Focusing on how a recipient might react or use your email takes extra work. It gives you, the sender, several more things to think about before dashing off an email. Oh, darn. It requires that you be more strategic when composing your message. By strategic, I mean you have to have a strategy for communicating what you need someone to do in a way that makes it easy (or at least easier) to do it. This makes email composition a little harder when you are learning how to do it, just like driving a car after you get your learner's permit. It also takes longer, like figuring out who has the right of way at four-way stops, at least at first. Accept this and move on.

Without a clear focus on the reader, the odds increase dramatically that your emails will be a stream of consciousness, making them hard for the reader to interpret and delaying the result you want. What do readers do if they don't understand what you want? Usually nothing, which is bad for you. If the action you want from others is not be clear or buried somewhere in rambling text, it will just sit in the recipient's inbox until they have time or motivation to untangle the mess you sent. Some busy people **never** have time for that, which does not bode well for getting what you wanted.

This book distinct from other email guides because it is based on a simple, memorable, and tightly integrated system. The system described in the book was accumulated from years of personal experience and learning about what works best. I have translated that experience into clear actions, strategies and tactics. You get to learn from my embarrassing gaffes and the crass mistakes made by others. I present practices that I have collected, experimented with, and tweaked over decades of high-volume personal and professional email. The practices will help you compose email messages that are easier for others to understand and act on. To help the ideas stick, there are many opportunities for practice. You will put the practices in action through the exercises.

What makes an email easy to understand and act on? What do people need to take action quickly and efficiently? Keep reading and you will learn. With practice using the checklists and tools of this book, the necessary thinking processes will become second nature very quickly.

What happens when your emails are easier to understand and process? You become a much more effective communicator. Your emails will get what you need faster. Those who get email from you will be much more efficient because of what you send them, and you will get into trouble less frequently (always a good thing). You will be so good at communicating in email that you will amaze friends, colleagues, and acquaintances. You will look like an Email Ninja to them. What's not to like about that?

Unlike becoming a martial arts Ninja, becoming an Email Ninja does not take decades of study and practice. It doesn't take great physical conditioning. It does take mental conditioning. It also takes the guidance of a sensei, an experienced teacher like me, and discipline to learn and follow the system explained in this book. Both guidance and discipline are essential. I didn't invent the term Email Ninja, but it is a compact way to describe a person that can use email with such great skill that it seems miraculous, even a delight, to recipients. This section defines what an Email Ninja is and why you should want to be one.

If you do an internet search for "email ninja" (I'll be right here when you finish ...), you will get lots of results and cute graphics. Most of the search results describe what Email Ninjas presumably do, not what one is. My definition of Email Ninja is **a person who focuses on readers to design highly effective emails to accomplish their goals**. An Email Ninja's primary aim is to provide readers the key information they need to act on email messages. An Email Ninja does not merely write or compose email, they *design* it using strategies tuned for specific types of messages. An Email Ninja is an expert at combining strategy with skilled execution in email.

The bottom line for becoming an Email Ninja is **it makes you more effective**. As email, instant messages, and other electronic communications proliferate in the inboxes of busy people, you need an edge for your messages to stand out. Making your communications concise, clear, and very specific is that edge. Like a hypnotist, you can draw people to your emails. You should design emails this way not just because it is a nice thing to do, but because it will help you get what you want faster.

Reasons for Becoming an Email Ninja

In case you are not convinced yet, here are specific reasons for becoming an Email Ninja:

• **Efficiency**: emails that concisely state the point, making it clear what action(s) are expected from readers are shorter and easier for them to understand and use.

• **Effectiveness**: when emails are easier for recipients to use, they are likely to generate the desired action(s) much more quickly. Communication is only effective when appropriate information is portrayed AND that information is correctly perceived by the recipient. I think Peter Drucker (1999) was spot on that communication is what happens in the mind of the recipient, "… it is the recipient who communicates" (Drucker, 1999, p. 391). He also wrote that "communications … have to start with the recipient rather than the emitter …" (Drucker, 1999, p. 491).

• **Fewer misunderstandings**: electronic communications are easy to write and send, hard to retract, and can be the source of lasting regret. Miscommunication and damage to one's credibility and reputation are big risks of poorly written emails. I have personally experienced the sting of both.

• **Professionalism**: good email skills convey an image of professionalism that is readily recognizable to readers.

The next section explains how the book is organized and provides an overview of its main ideas.

How the Book is Organized

Part 1 of the book, The System: Brilliant Email in Seven Steps, begins with an overview of strategies that lie behind the specific practices (Chapter 2-Introduction to the Email Strategies). It then proceeds through the seven steps, one chapter at a time, for composing brilliant emails. To make them more memorable, the steps are organized around the acronym PAASTUB. I wanted the acronym to be PAYSTUB, but that would have required me to use "Yahoos" or "Y-all" for Addressees. There are times when it feels like I am communicating with yahoos, but it just didn't set the right tone. A pay stub is a record of the monetary result for services rendered. In the same way, clear communications that accomplish your goals are the result of following the PAASTUB steps.

- Step 1, **Purpose** of the email (Chapter 3-Purpose is Clear).
- Step 2, **Action** clearly stated (Chapter 4-Action).
- Step 3, **Addressees** for whom your email adds value (Chapter 5-Addressees).
- Step 4, **Subjects** that are succinct and artful get results (Chapter 6-Subject at Art).
- Step 5, **Trash** and fluff complicate messages so take it out (Chapter 7-Take Out the Trash).
- Step 6, **Ugly** remarks need to be removed or edited to avoid offense or embarrassment (Chapter 8-Ugly Remarks Edited).
- Step 7, **Bottom** Line Up Front (BLUF), summarize the key points of your email in three sentences or less (Chapter 9-BLUF-ing).

Part 2 of the book is a collection of high leverage strategies and tactics for email.
- My minimalist approach to managing email and strategies for composing messages for specific situations (Chapter 10: Strategies for Specific Kinds of Emails).
- Useful tactics that apply across all email messages (Chapter 11: Tactics for High-Leverage Email).

Part 3 of the book is a collection of reference tools and templates that will help you learn the email system. They make it easier to adopt and internalize the practices (Chapter 12: Tools). It includes checklists, sample subject keywords, and customizable templates for recurring emails. Part 3 is a collection of the most important tools in the book, but not a complete restatement of the practices.

Part 4 of the book applies its principles of communication to text messaging. It is an Email Ninja's guide to the universe of text messaging. It is a single chapter (Chapter 13: An Email Ninja's Guide to Text Messaging) packed with ideas to improve your texting practices.

Part 5 is the conclusion of the book (Chapter 14: Final Thoughts). It lists the main idea of each chapter, the steps and the principles behind them, and provides final thoughts on using the system.

Each chapter of the book has a similar layout to make it easier to get the most out of it. Chapters begin with a BLUF, Bottom Line Up Front, that identifies the core ideas of the chapter. Next, the practices or strategies are explained. When applicable, there are exercises to practice the skills and deepen your understanding of them. A summary of the chapter's key points comes at the end of every chapter.

Taken individually, many of the practices of the book might look like "common sense," but they are so much more. If they really were common sense, then everybody would be using them. Strangely enough, they do not. What makes the book distinctive (and very useful) is the way the practices work together. The sum is much greater than the individual practices.

There are many ways to read this book to benefit from the ideas. Most readers will want to read the book straight through. Other readers can skim the BLUF and summary for each chapter to get a quick overview of the contents. This may be useful for familiarizing yourself with the contents, but be careful of doing too much skipping around or concluding "I know this" based on skimming the chapter BLUFs. To benefit from the system for communications explained in this book, you need to understand each practice and the principle behind it.

Each part of the book describes an important function for the system. Chapters 10 and 11 are especially significant. They unite all the practices explained in the previous chapters in a powerful way for the specific types of email messages people send most often. The next section describes in greater detail how to take advantage of the way this book is organized.

This book is written with readers in mind, just like your emails should be. The **BLUF** at the beginning of each chapter describes what you will learn from reading the chapter.

What is a BLUF? BLUF stands for Bottom Line Up Front. It is a very high leverage communications tool I learned from years of serving on military staffs. It means the same thing as "spill the beans early," which is common advice in business writing. It is different than a summary. People on military staffs and other organizations that prize efficiency are encouraged to boil down the contents of their messages to just a few sentences (Bottom Line) at the beginning (Up Front) of an email or memo. This text foreshadows what the memo or email is about and what is expected of readers in the first ten-seconds of reading. For people that get a lot of email (especially on mobile devices), reading a BLUF is super efficient. Busy people really like it when you get right to the point.

The BLUF conveys the essence of a communication in three, plus or minus one, sentences. Anytime your BLUF exceeds four sentences, it is not succinct enough. I actually received a memo from someone that had a BLUF that took up half the page! There was a training opportunity if ever I saw one. Think of the BLUF as a summary or abstract on a super dose of caffeine or, as Joe Friday from the U.S. television series "Dragnet" was wont to say, "Just the facts, ma'am." The chapter BLUFs of this book give readers a concise preview of the chapters.

WARNING for those in a super hurry to read the book: It is unlikely that reading the BLUFs alone will be sufficient to understand and practice the skills described in the chapters. In order to really grasp the material and gain the understanding necessary to unlearn the bad email habits you have accumulated, most people will need to read the entire chapter. The chapters are generally short and easy to digest. Reading the entire chapter will help you grasp the philosophy behind the practices. You will also see how the practices link to each other because I explicitly address this. The power of the book's system comes from how the practices link to and reinforce each other.

The **Introduction** to each chapter is a short explanation for why the material in the chapter is important in just a bit more detail than the

BLUF. The BLUF is a statement of *what* is in the chapter. The introduction explains *why* it is important.

The **Body** section of each chapter is where you will find the details of the skills and examples.

The **Practice** sections give you the opportunity to put the skills in action. The exercises are designed to give readers an opportunity to actually use the skills in the context of actual emails. Each exercise has an answer with my thought processes carefully explained. This way, you can compare it to your answer and thinking. For many of the practice exercises, there is no "right" answer, but some answers may be better than others. You decide.

The practice exercises will help you think differently about how you compose an email. The exercises are designed to stimulate thinking, which is why it is important that you not read the book before going to sleep at night. They may start the process of unlearning bad habits. Practicing skills makes them permanent. If you practice the skills, they can become a permanent part of your email routine.

The chapter **Summary** provides a succinct list of the key points covered in the chapter in bullet form. If you read the chapter BLUF then skip to the summary and see something that is surprising or confusing, this might be an indicator that you would benefit from reading the details in the body of the chapter. It also could be an indicator that you didn't know as much as you thought you did about the chapter contents.

As with many things, there are a myriad of ways you can use the practices, strategies, tactics, and tools of the system. It is my strong belief that the practices, strategies, tactics, and tools work best when used together. This is how it works for me and this is what many people have told me. They function collectively as an email approach that focuses on what the reader needs. All the parts of my system are mutually supportive to produce more effective communications. How? Because brief, clearly written emails with crisp subjects that instantly make the sender's purpose clear are what the **reader** needs to give you what **YOU** need. As you learn, internalize, and possibly tweak the system for your situation, the templates, tools, and examples help you execute the practices, strategies, and tactics more quickly and confidently. The email etiquette guide makes it easier to teach others how to adopt the same conventions. You can also recommend or buy copies of the book for them. For blatantly commercial reasons, I highly recommend this.

You *can* adopt or reject the recommended practices piecemeal, but I don't recommend it as a way to get the most from them. This book presents the systematic approach to email communications that I have found most effective at many organizations where I have worked and in my personal life. Great subjects are like good beer commercials featuring slightly dressed people at the beach. They grab recipient attention right away with mental images that are hard to ignore. However, what is the good of grabbing attention for a beer that doesn't taste good (i.e., provide what the user wants)? To become an Email Ninja, you have to compose the body of an email in a way that makes it really easy for recipients to accept the meeting request, provide the file, introduce you to someone, or provide the information you need. Isn't this obvious? It may be, but it takes some strategy to do it well because, if my email inbox is any indication, most people don't do it well. Beer brewers collect mountains of data to know who their potential customers are and relentlessly target them with their messages. This is like email addressing and making sure your message is optimally designed for just the recipients that need it. Beer commercials are often designed around a common theme with slight variations to convey a consistent message about their product. Creating email templates for common emails that you send accomplishes the same thing. I don't drink much beer, but I have noticed how effectively it is advertised.

Having an email etiquette guide for your group or organization may seem unnecessary. I assure it is not. Such a guide is a straightforward, succinct way to communicate your exceptions for crisp email communications. An etiquette guide is also a good way to remind people of the standard you expect when they stray. And they will certainly stray. You can count on that. All of the parts of my systematic approach to email function together to improve what comes into your inbox from your most frequent senders and enhance your ability to use email to get things done.

I strongly encourage you to use the practice sections of each chapter to get experience applying the skills. Practice is what will make you an Email Ninja, not just reading the book. Do the practice exercises when you are alert, focused, and have time to think carefully about the skill they target and not while watching beer commercials.

Key points from Chapter 1

- The guiding principle for email communications in this book is: focus on the reader. Give your email readers the information they need to understand what you want and how to prioritize getting it to you. This is easy to say, but it having a system really helps and practicing with that system leads to doing it consistently and effectively.
- An Email Ninja is a person who integrates strategies and skills to compose and manage emails that accomplish his or her goals quickly and efficiently.
- The reason for becoming an Email Ninja is that it helps you become more effective. Becoming an Email Ninja helps you communicate more clearly and get faster responses. An Email Ninja uses practices that will be greatly appreciated by their readers.
- Communication is what happens in the mind of the receiver, not in your mind and not on your screen.
- This book provides a system for writing and addressing emails to accomplish the most common email tasks.
- The strategies and tactics in the book reflect a systematic approach to communication that work. I have developed and taught this collection of lessons, ideas, practices, and tips to many others.
- Email etiquette is a set of rules and behavioral conventions that identify some behaviors as appropriate or inappropriate. An email etiquette guide serves as a standard for the kind of email expected in your organization or group. An email etiquette guide can help remind people of the standard when, not if, they stray.
- Each chapter of the book has a similar layout. It begins with the BLUF of the chapter. The skills or strategies are explained. There may be exercises to practice the skills. A summary at the end of the chapter identifies the key points in more detail than the BLUF, just like this list.

In Part 1 that follows, I describe the seven PAASTUB steps for composing and sending awesome emails. The PAASTUB steps will help you be more effective at accomplishing your goals. Each of the steps of my systematic approach to email work with the others like the carefully designed parts of a race car engine to enhance your ability to get things done. Now, move on to chapter 2 and review the components of the PAASTUB engine.

Part 1 The System: Seven Steps for Brilliant Email

Why are there 7 steps in your email system?

Because 8 was too many.

Chapter 2-Introduction to the Seven Steps

BLUF: The seven steps for constructing effective emails help you create communications with clear actions, text that is easy to read, and avoid embarrassing gaffes. The steps are a better mental flow for composing emails. The acronym PAASTUB makes them more memorable while you learn to compose better emails with a process that is more aligned to the way you think.

Introduction

Email is a wonderful, low-friction, informal, fast way to communicate. This chapter describes how to produce better email messages with a more effective composition "flow" enabled by the seven steps of my system. It will review some of the more significant benefits and costs of email that the system addresses and leverages, discuss how the process flow of most email programs can channel thinking inefficiently, and the flow for composing a highly effective email. Because we're just getting started, the chapter has no practice section.

Email has removed much of the friction that exists in more formal communications like letters and physical memos. This is a dual edged sword. On the benefit side, it is faster and easier to send communications to large numbers of people any time of day. Email usually does not require permission. Once you have their email addresses, sending a message to fifty people requires little more effort than sending it to one. On the cost side, anyone, anywhere, can try to put something in your inbox (thank goodness for spam filters), demand your attention, and require *you* to decide whether their message is relevant. Many emails, even those from colleagues, require lots of mental effort and time to determine their relevance or find the action.

Except for the subject (more about that in Chapter 6) and the sender, one email looks just like any other in your inbox. This impacts your ability to discriminate among the messages by size, shape, sender's address (unless you know them), and other physical characteristics like you can with physical mail. I don't even open physical mail unless it comes from a sender I recognize or feels like it contains a credit card (don't throw those away!). For physical mail, one of the clearest "throw this away without opening" markers is text like "time sensitive material" printed on the envelope. You may be sending similar indicators in the email messages you send. In the next section, I deconstruct the typical email composition process flow so I can reconstruct it later.

The Process Flow of Regular Email

All email programs have a "process flow" for creating messages even if you aren't aware of it. This section describes the typical process flow in some detail so you can understand how poorly aligned most email programs are to the way you actually think about communicating. Once that is clear, you will be able to understand how these programs lead you to produce poorly composed messages without thinking about it.

In the business world, process flow refers to path a product or service takes from raw material or customer request to the finished product. This flow for message composition has been codified into program design. An Email Ninja needs to be fully aware of all aspects of the message composition process. That's what this section is about.

When you begin composing a new message, the process flow proceeds from top to bottom after you open a new message window: addressees, priority, subject, attachments, message text, send. I will review each in turn to identify where the process is broken and lay the groundwork for the PAASTUB system that I believe is the remedy.

For new messages, addressing starts in a blank field and blinking cursor at the top of the window. Suppose your purpose is to send information about a call you are planning so people can prepare. Assume you have already verified that the attendees are available (more on this in Chapter 11). Since the cursor is already blinking at you in the address field, this suggests that choosing recipients comes first. How can it come before you know what you want to say? How do you know who needs to know what you have to say before you write it?

Choosing recipients can be complicated. Who should be To and who should be Cc? Should anyone be Cc? Why should anyone not invited to the meeting be informed about the fact that the meeting is happening? How can you be sure you invite all the **required** people? Just what is Bc anyway? This is a lot of mental work before you have written your first sentence!

For replies, the address field is already filled depending on whether you elect to reply to the sender or "all." Addressing emails is so taxing for some people that they set their default email reply behavior to reflexively "reply to all" for every single message they send. As you will learn in Chapter 5, I think this is an incredibly bad practice. Using "reply to all" for every single email should be accompanied by the same kind of nagging warnings you get when you leave the address field blank: "are you sure you want to reply to every single addressee with your insignificant issue?" "Are you sure you want to irritate so many people?" My favorite would be "Do you really have to be THAT lazy?"

For some email programs, the next step is to designate the priority of the message. The options for choosing importance can generate another set of complex questions. Is the importance of your message low, routine, or high? What if it is "super high"? If you are setting up a meeting, why would anyone come if it is of low importance? Is "low importance" the same as "not important" like emails about bake sales? If you send an email message that has low importance, does it mean that you don't care whether people read it? What is the difference between something that is routine and something that is low importance? Who decides that?

Subject is up next in the top to bottom composition sequence. Uh oh. You opened the new message window with only the vaguest idea of what you wanted to write like "I want to tell attendees the agenda for our call." Before you could start thinking about how that translates to a subject, you were immediately vectored away to addressing and message importance. Your brain began filling up rapidly, you started thinking about checking Facebook updates, you were alerted to new messages in your inbox, and you started losing track of what you wanted to write. After checking Facebook and the latest "Save the Date" email, you are probably really impatient to start writing the text of the message. You have lots of other things to work on, calls to make, and meetings to attend after sending the message so you want to "get on with it."

The email program doesn't care about your schedule or how much work you have. It still presents you with that blank subject field and blinking cursor beckoning you to type something, anything so you can move on. What was your reason for composing the message before you got distracted by addressing it? In this example, which you have probably forgotten already, the email was about the meeting you are planning. You want to get on to explaining why the meeting is important, the agenda, your goals, etc. At this point, you are running low on brain capacity. You could also be suffering from acute caffeine deficit. Your priority is not creating a subject that will be helpful to recipients. You just want this mental torture to end so you can start composing the message so you start looking for mental shortcuts. A common practice at this point is to just use the first subject that comes to mind: "meeting." While possibly common, this is a terrible practice, but email programs aren't judgmental. Unlike your recipients, they don't care what you type.

Some people are so impatient to start writing the email, overcome by mental blocks, or distracted by attachments that they skip the subject field entirely. They think, "I don't know what this message is really about. I haven't written it yet. I don't want to use a lame subject like "meeting" so I'll come back to the subject later." Except they don't. They send the dreaded "No subject" email.

Some email programs let you attach files whenever you want. Certainly you have some files that will provide helpful background, but you have to find them first. Where are they are on your computer? Are they in "documents," "desktop," or in an email message that someone already sent you? What were their filenames and in what folder are they located? Once you find the files and attach them, you can relax. You have avoided the "no file attached" gaffe. Whew! Should you mention the attachments in the body of the email? Should you? Did you specifically identify how readers will find the attachments useful or necessary? Probably not. Why bother? They can open the attachments and see for themselves, right?

The process is slightly different if you are replying or forwarding the email. While addressing is still a chore, you don't have to give any thought to the subject. Hurray! If you are replying to or forwarding a message, all email systems default to the original subject. It doesn't matter how bad that subject was or even if it was blank. Ha! That was the other person's fault. You don't even have to think about it. The email system is ignorant of whether your reply is on track or goes off in a completely new direction so you can use the original subject no matter how irrelevant it is now.

The second difference for replies or forwards is how much of the original text to include. If the meeting is related to a series of previous emails, should you include all the text from all the previous replies, including everyone else's lengthy email signatures and all the prior addressees of each message? Maybe. The recipients might find something useful in all that text even if you didn't. Be honest, you didn't read all that stuff anyway. Maybe they will. Besides, it would be a lot of work to read through the tedious collection of replies and forwards and remove all the messages that just consisted of forwards and "FYI." You don't have time for that and it could be useful "context." The message recipients can figure out what's important.

Pause briefly to consider all the mental effort and decisions you had to make just to be *ready to start* composing the body of the email: addressing, importance, subject, and attachments. Now you confront the ocean of white space in the box for the message body and you are starting to get mentally fatigued and seasick. You were probably interrupted several times during the process by coworkers needing help, phone calls, new email message notifications, and FaceBook or Twitter updates about which of your friends are eating what kind of soup. You *know* you look at all those.

Despite all the interruptions and decisions, you have to get the message written so just keep going. As you begin to compose it, what do you want to say? Do you have an outline? Have you written any notes for organizing your thoughts? As you read this paragraph, you may be thinking, "An outline for an email? Written notes? Is he serious?" You may also be thinking that you would spend more time writing the outline than it would take to send the email, right? Email is informal and quick. People send email message shortly after thoughts pop into their heads. No one writes outlines anymore, especially not for something quick like email. How do I know this? I don't know it exactly, but it seems likely from the rambling, disorganized, stream of consciousness emails I get in my inbox.

If you don't write an outline, the first opportunity for you to see what you wanted to say is after you type the email message. Your ideas for the meeting and what support you need from attendees will probably just start pouring out of your head into the message. This makes for a tangled, rambling message.

As you see what you have written, possibly in one long stream of consciousness since you didn't use an outline, your ideas are much clearer to you and now you have a much better idea of what the meeting is about. That's a relief. Will your message recipients have this same clarity about the meeting from the content you just provided? Who knows? You are probably not thinking about them anyway. It was enough trouble to get all your ideas for the meeting out of your head and into the email message. You are starting to get really mentally fatigued now. To the extent you think about the message recipients at all, you may blithely assume that reading through the text of your message will make the meeting purpose and necessary preparations as clear to them as they are to you.

Are you ready to send or should you think about shortening that really long email signature if you are sending the email strictly to people within the organization that already know you well. Like the thoughtlessness of "reply all," you probably don't think about whether you should include an email signature that includes your name, job title, phone numbers, emails, current interests, and pithy quotes from Mother Theresa and Socrates to advertise your philosophies of life and work. You created an email signature so you don't *have* to think about it.

At the bottom of the message you typed, the one that took you much longer to write than you expected when you first thought "I should send an email about this" is the "send" button, usually highlighted. It beckons you like a Siren, "Just press me and move on to other work." This is hard to resist.

Are you ready to hit send? Is it worth the time to re-read and edit your stream of consciousness to make sure you included all the information your readers need? Does the subject bear any resemblance to the content of the email message? Re-read and edit an email? Review the subject? Who does those things? Email is only slightly more formal than text messages that start with "Whazzuup?", right

Are you concerned about appearing ignorant if the message is riddled with misspellings, bad grammar, and typos? Heck no, it is just for internal distribution anyway! No re-reading, just hit send and move on to the next message in your box or high priority task.

What a mess! Even if I slightly exaggerated, this is the process you go through *every time* they send an email. Even though you may not be aware that all this is going on, you probably noticed many things in the narrative that apply to you.

How much do you think of the process you use for sending email? There is a better way. You don't have to let a programmer lead you down a dark alley of muddled communications practices. You don't have to compose emails top to bottom just because the email client is designed that way. This book is about putting you in charge of the way you write emails that so you can provide recipients what is most useful to them to accomplish your goals more effectively. The next section describes email process flow based on my seven steps for better email.

The Process Flow of an Email Ninja

Regardless of the email tool you use, I believe that the best email message is clear about your purpose; succinctly states the action you want and when you need it; conveys the most important information in the first two lines; uses a subject that makes the message content clear *without having to open the message*, and is only sent *after* a final review for alignment between purpose, action, brevity, and recipients. I divided the process flow to consistently produce emails like this into seven steps that begin with the most important parts first:

- **Purpose is Clear**-get the purpose of the message clear in your head before you write the message. Do you want action from someone? Do you need information? Are you giving information? Are you setting up a meeting? These are the primary reasons for sending an email message.

- **Action**-what is the action you want from your recipient? State what you want and when you want it in the first two lines of the message. If you are providing information, what is most important for others to know? How are you adding something *they will value* for their work?

- **Addressees**-*who* is going to derive value from your email message? This is very important. Who needs to know about or read your email because it adds value to the work they do? Value is a very high bar for choosing who gets the message. It means your message will *change the work they do*. It doesn't mean that it might be useful for them in some cosmic sense like knowing the earth orbits the sun (very cosmic). Unless you think your message will change someone's work, don't make them an addressee. This means "reply to all" is not a valid option most of the time. People are already getting more than enough emails without having to read your email to learn that it doesn't apply to them.

- **Subject as Art**-make the subject of your email GREAT. Once you are clear about the purpose of your email, you can draft a preliminary, great subject. Because the purpose should help you formulate greater clarity about what you need, when you need it, the priority of the communication, and who needs to know, NOW is the time to make a great subject that conveys all that in the subject alone. A great subject is the most important part of the email. It is your best chance for your message to get priority over the scores of emails that people get each day.

- **Take Out the Trash**-remove extraneous information from the message that is likely to distract people from getting the information they need quickly, especially on mobile devices with small screens.

- **Ugly Remarks Edited**-you should avoid sending email with "sensitive" information whenever you can. This is not about state or company secrets, but rather anything that can get you into trouble later. This applies just as well to emails you forward from others. Edit or delete intemperate comments of others before sending.
- **BLUF**-when you do your final read through of the message, take a final look at the BLUF to make sure it aligns with the content of the message and the subject, conveying the appropriate mix of brevity and clarity in the first one to two lines of the email.

The seven steps spell the "word" **PAASTUB** (pronounced "paystub") to make them easier to remember. The steps are a useful way to teach the concepts of good email practice, but do not have to be performed in a strict, top down sequence. As you will learn in subsequent chapters, you can and should go back and forth between the steps in the process of composing great emails as you gain clarity about what you are trying to communicate.

The remaining chapters of Part I explain the flow of producing emails in terms of the PAASTUB seven steps, provide the philosophy behind each step, and give opportunities to practice the steps when possible.

Key points from Chapter 2

- The seven steps reflect a better process flow for composing emails than what is built into email programs. Take control of the process so it works for you.
- You should get better results and send clearer emails using the seven steps because they seem to account for the way your brain works better than other approaches.
- The seven steps do not have to be finished in order. Some back and forth between steps is completely acceptable and actually desirable because the steps reinforce and improve each other.

The next chapter describes the first step of the PAASTUB process, making the purpose clear. This is the foundation for writing effective email messages.

Chapter 3-Step 1: Purpose is Clear

BLUF: Being clear in your own mind about why you are sending an email is the first step for making that purpose clear to your readers. Most email falls into four basic types: meeting requests, event announcements, questing action, taking action. Your ability to accomplish one of the four purposes is enhanced by tactics tailored to each purpose.

Introduction

Clarity of purpose is essential to produce a well-composed email message. At the most elemental level possible, the purpose of an email is either providing information or requesting action from a recipient. Information being provided could be results of a meeting, research, something that was requested, or a file to read. Action requested could be time on their calendar, information, money, or some other concrete action. This chapter begins with the principle behind step 1, Purpose is Clear, continues with how clarity of purpose evolves in the process of writing an email message, and describes the four fundamental types of email messages to set up the strategies applicable to each. These strategies will be detailed in the remainder of Part 1 and later in Part 2.

A Clear Purpose is Necessary for Effective Email

The principle behind step 1, Purpose is Clear, is that a clear purpose is necessary for effective email. Before you can convey your thoughts clearly to recipients, the purpose of your email message needs to be clear to you. Asking yourself, possibly out loud (as long as no one can hear you), "what do I want?" is a good way to start getting the clarity you need. Another way to think of this is: what outcome do you hope to achieve by sending the email? If the answer you give is more than a single sentence, think harder or consider sending more than one message (see Chapter 11, Single Topic).

The best way to start with either giving or receiving something is having clarity on what your purpose is for doing it. That's what Purpose is Clear is all about. If you are asking for something in an email, make sure to state when you need it. Depending on how familiar the recipient is with the issues associated with the action, you may have to provide background information to support the action.

Don't be surprised if your purpose for sending the message changes through composing it. Many times, the clarity of your thinking about the purpose of an email message will improve through writing it. You may begin composing your email by thinking that you just want to provide information, but realize during the writing process that what you really want is *feedback* on the information, which is action. Any email that asks readers to do something is an action email. This happens to me all the time. Composing the email, imagining what the readers need, reading, and re-reading what you have written will naturally sharpen your thinking. You can't really know what you think about something until you see what you have written about it. As you re-read the email message a few times before sending it (see Chapter 11, Final Review), you will revisit your purpose, find typos (of course), and think of better ways to organize your ideas. This is a normal part of the writing process, but neglected far too often judging from the tangled messes of text that arrive in my inbox all the time.

There are four basic purposes for sending an email:
- Meeting or event invitations and announcements (when you know the time and date already)
- Meeting or event set up (finding a time and date depending on others' availability, providing information to support the meeting)
- Giving something

- Information in the body of an email
- Information in attachments
- Comments on someone else's email
- Asking for something
  - Request for help
  - Feedback on something
  - Asking a question
  - Action (by a deadline)

These purposes or types of emails may strike you as obvious. "So what?" might be your reaction. Since nearly every email you send will will be one of these types, thinking in terms of these types will help you focus on what you need to do to accomplish your purpose. For example, if you want someone to take action, you should think about exactly what they need to take the action as quickly and easily as possible. Gaining clarity for your purpose for sending the email is important because you should use different strategies for the subject, body text, and addressees for each. These strategies will be addressed in subsequent chapters.

Practice

In the example emails below (taken from an actual inbox with slight edits to shield the guilty from embarrassment), identify which of the four basic types (meeting invitation, meeting set up, information, asking for something) it is. If it looks like more than one type, note each type. If the email text requests action, note how many actions are requested.

Practice 1

Dear all,
We have decided to launch a picture gallery on the website (link). Check it out. I encourage you to look at the pictures and provide feedback.

Answer: email type is asking for something (one action)

Practice 2

We returned from Australia. Do you have time to talk on the phone this Friday or next (or days in between)?

Answer: information and meeting set up

Practice 3

This is Doctor Ralph Soule checking in and letting you know that I am available to answer questions. I also have a blog that you might find useful, especially the post about X.

Answer: information

Practice 4

I've just returned from 10 days of business travel and lost my voice! Would you mind if we rescheduled our call for sometime next week? Please let me know which dates and times might work best for you.

We have decided to launch a picture gallery on the website (link). Check it out. I encourage you to look at the pictures and provide feedback.

Answer: meeting setup (first action), information (second action)

Practice 5

I've done some research and put together a document that I would like you to review. Please recommend any changes you think are in order.

Answer: asking for something (two actions, read and recommend changes)

Key points from Chapter 3

• The first step of the PAASTUB process, Purpose Clear, means be clear about your reason for sending an email before composing it. You cannot make your purpose clear to someone else if is it not clear to you.

- The principle behind step 1, Purpose is Clear, is that a clear purpose is necessary for effective email.
- Thinking in terms of four basic types of email helps you think more clearly about how to write your message. The types are:: meeting invitations, meeting setup, giving something, or asking for something.
- Don't worry that your purpose for sending the email may change in the process of writing it. The final review described in Chapter 11 gives you the opportunity to make sure your message is still organized effectively to accomplish the new purpose.

Conveying the action of an email clearly and succinctly is the focus of the next chapter. The next step of the PAASTUB process is the action or what you want people to *do* after reading your email message.

Chapter 4-Step 2: Action-What and When?

BLUF: Make what you need and when you need it really, really clear in your email messages. If you are just providing information, clearly state so and what you expect people to do with it. Use the subject to telegraph the action or information. Stating the action clearly in your message makes it easier for recipients to decide if they can give you what you need and prioritize getting it to you.

Introduction

The second step in the PAASTUB email process is to be crystal clear about the Action you want and when you want it. This is important because the first question that comes to mind when really busy people read email message is, "What do I have to do?" The second question is mostly likely, "Do I have time to do this?" The purpose of achieving clarity on what you need and when you need it is to make it as easy as you can for your recipient to answer the "Do I have time for this action?" question. This chapter addresses the principle behind step 2, Action, the key elements of action clarity, communicating actions to non-native speakers of your language, examples of action clarity for specific types of email messages, and some considerations for choosing your action due date.

Make the Action Clear

The principle behind step 2, Action, is to make it easy for your email message readers to know what you want by when. The first two lines (not sentences) of the email should be what you want and when you need it. Don't bury the action in the middle at the bottom of your email. If you are not asking for anything, then the first two lines should state the value you expect the reader to derive from what you are sending. Don't worry if this seems too abrupt. It is not abrupt, it is both helpful and considerate of your readers' limited time and attention. Your readers will appreciate your skill at getting to the point quickly.

A proper action statement succinctly describes who needs what by when, in a single sentence if possible. The elements of action clarity are: who (be specific), what the action is, and the date it is needed. The content of the action answers "what needs to be done, exactly?" Is it a recommendation? Feedback on a document? Calling or emailing someone? For example, if you want something written, be specific about points to address, format, and length. Try to imagine yourself being asked to do what you are requesting and answer all the questions *you* might have. The better you can anticipate relevant questions from the action party, the more likely they will meet your requirements. They might also be impressed by your efficiency and thoughtfulness, but don't count on it.

Special caution is in order when communicating with people that are not native speakers of your language. In this case, creating action clarity is an even more important so it doesn't get lost in translation. Your first priority is to keep your language very basic and concrete, avoiding complex, technical, or ambiguous expressions whenever you can. If you are doing mission cooperation with another country's space agency, as NASA did with the French, using technical terms is unavoidable. Just makes sure there is a common understanding of what they mean. You could do this providing definitions at the bottom of the email message. Another option when you have to use complex, technical terms with non-native speakers of your language is to add a native speaker of the other language to your local team. This person can provide insight into how the message and action might be interpreted before you send it. Depending on the need for specialized technical knowledge, you might want to embed a member of the other team locally with yours and not depend on email alone for communications, but that's beyond the scope of this book.

Questions to address for producing maximum action clarity are easier to illustrate with some specific examples:

If you want a recommendation, be specific about the position you seek and which of your talents you want emphasized. You could include a portion of the job description with the email. What format and length should the recommender use? Is there a template or form that is required or can it be a letter? If a letter, to whom is the letter addressed at what address? Does the organization requiring the recommendation require anything specific addressed? If so, provide that list. Is the recommendation electronic or will it be sent in the mail? If electronic, what file format should be used and where should it be sent or uploaded? If it will arrive in the mail, provide an estimate for when it will arrive.

If you want comments on something you have written, tell the person exactly what to comment on. Closing your email with a cryptic "comments?" line just before your signature does not focus on the reader. A vague request for comments IS NOT AN ACTION, it is a study problem. Study problems sent via email are bad. I discuss this in more detail in Chapter 10.

State the goals for your document or email text when you ask for comments. What do you want to know? This may help readers give you more useful comments. Do you want a quick reaction or something more thorough? Did you struggle with one part of the text and need help? Which part was it? Do you want the reviewer to recommend alternate text?

When someone sends me an email with "comments?" near the bottom, I send a quick reply "I want to help, but am confused about the action you want. It would really help me focus if I knew specifically what you want to know and when you need it." I shouldn't have to guess about this-just don't say that in the reply. The tone of a reply like this is crucial. It focuses on what *I need* and not on what *they didn't do*. It is a request for help, not a rebuke. Not only are you asking for clarity, but you are clearly indicating that you want to help them. Unless the person that sent the original email is clueless (alas, they are out there), they will get the subtle message that' you won't replay to emails that finish with "comments?" If they are clueless, you can't fix that with an email reply.

Are you inviting people to collaborate on a document? How long should the document be? Does the order of contribution matter? Do you want specific people to work on sections or should everyone to work on the entire thing? Do you want contributors to notify the group when they have added or modified text?

If you are asking more than one question, collect them all in one place. Precede the question block with "I need to know these things" or something similar. This is addressed in more detail in Chapter 11.

Choosing the date you need the action completed involves some strategy. Never give the action party the latest date possible or you are likely to get burned by people that miss the date. Request the action a few days or a week in advance of the *real* date in case you process the data or don't get what you need from the person the first time. Requesting completion of the action a few days early also helps you manage unforeseeable problems like power outages, garbage can fires, and meetings announced five minutes before they start. Clear action dates help the other person make space in their schedule for what *they* have to do to take the action.

Some readers might think it is rude or too abrupt to start an email with the action they want. Thus begin of their action emails with several paragraphs describing recent activities and matters of personal interest, putting the action at the end of the message. Don't do this. An email with action is NOT a greeting card. Greeting cards have pretty graphics, some pithy message, and   personal message below the message. You are not sending a personal update, you want the recipient to DO something. It is actually more polite and respectful of someone's time to begin the email message with a brief statement of what you want and when. By all means provide a personal update, but at the very bottom of the email message.

The next section gives you the opportunity to assess actual action requests that I have received. Do they provide enough information so you could take the action requested? You make the call.

Practice

Based on the example action requests (taken from my inbox with slight edits), ask yourself if the action is clear enough to take action. If you think you would need more information to take the action requested, what would it be?

Practice 1

I would appreciate your recommendation for the job with this firm. My interview is scheduled for April 30. The job solicitation focuses on [list of some a specific tasks].

What questions would you ask?

Answer: What's the   format for the recommendation and when is it needed? How long should it be? Where do I send it? Do I address it to a specific person? What should I focus on?

Practice 2

I have registered for the conference and plan to walk the Camino Primitivo prior. Would it be possible to store my conference clothing with someone or in some location around 29 March and pick it up just before the conference?

What questions would you ask?

Answer: Exactly where and when will the person arrive to drop off their things?

Practice 3

The hospital changed my father's cardiology appt to 6 Feb 1320. I will be out of town. Can you take him? The heart clinic is adjacent to the hospital on Acme Blvd.

What questions would you ask?

Answer: The address of the hospital unless you already know what it is. How early are patients required to arrive for appointments? Is there anything that needs to be brought to the appointment?

Key points from Chapter 4

- The second step of the PAASTUB process, Action, requires you to be as specific as possible about what you want and when you want it.
- The goal of the completing the Action step is to answer all

questions the recipient might have about the action they need to take: who does what by when.

- When you are the one taking the action, make it clear that you have addressed the actions from the original email. Re-read the original email as many times as needed to collect all the actions.

The next chapter illuminates the importance of having clarity about the addressees of an email.

Chapter 5-Step 3: Addressees

BLUF: Only send email to recipients that need to know the content. The Addressees of your email message should only be the people who will be truly grateful for receiving it. Use the Cc: field of email sparingly. Do not automatically "reply to all." Make it clear why new people are being added to an ongoing email discussion.

Introduction

Step 3 of the PAASTUB process, Addressees, is about deliberately focusing on who needs to know what's in your email and why they need to know it. This is important because you should only send email to people that *need* to know what you have to say lest you clutter other inboxes. This chapter describes the problem with thoughtless email addressing, some assumptions about why some people use "reply to all" for every darn email they send, the confusion that "reply to all" can create for who has action, suggests guidelines for telling others what they need to know, and offers some tips when you're unsure who your audience should be (it happens).

Keep Just the Right People Informed

The principle behind Step 3 Addressees is keep the right people informed. Using the "To" field is something that most people grasp intuitively. "To" parties need to take some kind of action based on the email. The carbon copy ("Cc") field is more subtle and actually takes more thought to use effectively to prevent cluttering other people's inboxes with junk. It takes more thought because using it skillfully **requires** you to spend time thinking about answers to questions like "Why is this message useful to someone that has no action?"

You should think of focusing on a narrow set of addressees for your message as your contribution to making the world a better place, like not throwing trash out your car window. Sending email to people that can't take action or won't be affected and thus don't need to know is bad behavior. Just because you couldn't be bothered to think about how to address your email or you wanted to "just be safe" is no excuse to clutter their inboxes with trash that adds no value for them. That's right, trash. Is trash too strong here? What about blockheads that "reply to all" when meeting announcements are sent to a large group? We know who know you are! If you cannot attend the meeting because of your dog's pedicure appointment, NO ONE needs to know except the meeting arranger! This is just SPAM to everyone else.

An Email Ninja focuses communication on just the people that will derive important value from it. By important value, I mean: there is action for them, there is reason to believe that they will do or think about things differently in the future based the message contents, or someone important in the organization might ask them about it. This sets a very high bar for your email addressees.

For meeting invitations sent to a group, you *never* reply to all about whether you can attend unless the organizer asks you to do so. If you have concerns about some part of the message, it is more appropriate to address your reply to a smaller set of addressees than the original group. The considerate thing to do is "reply to all" *just once* to request this discussion and ask for interested parties to contact *just you* if they think they should be included.

Some email senders abdicate their responsibility to determine the addressees who need to know about their email. They give themselves away because they use "reply to all" for every darn email they send. You always know when *they* cannot be on the group phone call even when the information has no value for you. The email system set up feature that allows users to use "reply to all" as the default mode should carry a warning label: WARNING-BAD PRACTICE (in large red letters).

Replying "to all" without any thought definitely simplifies the email addressing and makes things easier for the sender. It simplifies what you have to think about when you reply, a practice psychologists call "reducing cognitive load." Wearing the same clothes to the office every day does the same thing. Just be sure to wash them periodically if you do this.

The reflexive "reply to all" practice is both curious and interesting. I wonder at the motivation and the reasoning process people used to decide that mindlessly replying to all makes sense. While it makes *their* lives easier, it just complicates everyone else's. I have confronted people a few times about replying to all with trivial responses and I didn't learn very much. In one case, I replied to a junior member of the organization with the message "I don't wish to be rude, but can you help me understand why everyone on the email distribution needs to know about your inability to attend the meeting?" The reply I received was "I'm sorry. I didn't mean to do that." I wonder. The brainless "reply to all" phenomenon occurs way too frequently for it just to be an accident.

When I have asked why they do it, no one has ever given me what would probably be the most honest answer for replying "to all" all the time. That would be something like, "I default to 'reply to all' because it is easier for me. My time is too valuable to bother thinking about email addressing. I don't spend any time thinking about how it impacts others."

In a better world, this this pernicious practice could be stopped cold. Organizations would just have to require that people get permission from their bosses to "reply to all" as the default addressing option for emails. I can dream that this would require people to prove that they could responsibly manage this feature before being turned loose to annoy the rest of us. But probably not.

There is an antidote to being included in a very active email discussion that has no relevance to you. Simply ask to be removed as an addressee. I've done this and seen others do it. A short reply with the text "Please take me off distribution for these emails" is usually sufficient to restore a micro-level of sanity to your email inbox. It might make members of the active discussion pause for a millisecond to think more carefully about email addressing. But don't get your hopes up.

You can specifically note in your original message whether reply to all is appropriate. This could be your one contribution to a better email world. It is very easy to do. At the top of your original email, the last sentence of the Bottom Line Up Front (see Chapter 9), include something brief like "Please don't reply to all with your response."

Some people, especially leaders, may tolerate or encourage indiscriminate use of "reply to all" out of fear they will miss important information. This is certainly a risk, but I don't believe that having an inbox cluttered with trivia is worth it. When are they going to have time to read all the clutter anyway?

Leaders should inform their teams about what they need to be kept informed about. This is not hard and I did it every time I reported to a new organization. Just send an email to the team, "subject: keeping me informed," that lists the top five or so things that are important for you to know. This may change from time to time so review the list to keep it up to date for your latest projects and priorities. If someone gets carried away and starts informing you of things you don't need to know, thank them and *gently* inform them that they can stop. As I note in Chapter 11, Criticize Gently, face-to-face is the best way to provide any negative feedback.

If you want to be taken of distribution of a very active email topic, replying with "Please take me off distribution for these emails" is probably too curt. The people doing all the replaying back and forth in your inbox are probably trying to do the right thing. They just are so focused on what they are discussing that they're note thinking about you. If you are a senior leader and can't tell them in person, you can send something like "Ralph, I appreciate the emails you have been sending me about this issue. It looks like you have the situation under control so you don't need to send me any more emails on this topic unless you have a problem or need my help." Another approach is "It looks like this is an important conversation to have, but I am not sure how I can help. Unless you need action from me, please take me off distribution." The gentle approach is appropriate because you want inbox sanity but you don't want to discourage people from informing you when they think it is necessary. Curt replies just rub people the wrong way.

One equally reflexive and risky response to thoughtless "reply to all" or abuse of the cc field is to inform your staff that you will only read emails specifically addressed to you. I cannot say whether this is effective in reducing inbox clutter or keeps you better informed of important things. It does strike me as drastic and it could come across as condescending. I have obtained good results with reducing unnecessary use of the cc field by publishing an email etiquette policy and reminding people when they stray from the guidelines. I have included an email etiquette template as one of the tools in this book.

Indiscriminate use of the cc field can create confusion unless the text of the email makes it clear who is supposed to act on the message. Senders might assume this is clear from context when it isn't. While it may be true that the action party is obvious, why leave it to chance or create a puzzle for recipients?

Copying people on important email communications does have its place in the PAASTUB process. Here are some specific instances when it is useful to receive an email even though no action is assigned to you.

- The originator works for you and you want to stay informed on an important project they are managing, like providing support for an important customer with a problem. It is doubtful that you need to read everything they are doing and all the replies they get related to a project, but it is possible depending on the importance of the project and experience level of the person managing it.
- The originator has experienced a problem or is dealing with a sensitive issue that could have significant repercussions for the organization or group. Being on the recipient list will alert you right away if one of the action addressees has a problem.
- The content of the email may impact someone that works with you. You may know who these people are better than the sender does so you can connect them with the sender for future communications.
- Your boss may get a phone call or email from someone senior based on the message. In this case, copy your boss *after* you have talked to him or her.
- It is important or useful for the action addressees of an email to have an indication that you are aware of an issue. Just having your email address appear in the cc field is not proof that you are informed, but it is a common assumption people make. If you have coached members of your team on your priorities for being informed and to use the system of this book, you can stay informed on a topic by briefly scanning the

emails related to it, possibly from the subjects alone.

- The information in the email is significant enough that you *might* take action in response to it. The action could include calling someone, requesting a meeting, asking for more information, or telling a superior.

What if you are not sure who should be informed? If you are not sure who needs to be apprised of the contents of your email, do not default to informing everyone you can think of. Make an educated guess about who should be copied and ask them to help you identify anyone else that needs to know. Use some standard text like, "If anyone recognizes that I left someone important off this email, please add them and let me know so I can fix that." If you are concerned that you included people that don't need to know, you can add text like, "I made some assumptions about who needs to be informed about [state the topic] and put them on the cc line. If I was incorrect, please let me know and I will remove you from future emails."

Sample text useful for getting emails sent just to the people that will derive important value from them. I have collected all the samples from the chapter text here, for convenience, and added a few more.

- "I don't wish to be rude, but can you help me understand why everyone on the email distribution needs to know about your inability to attend the meeting?"
- "Unless you need something from me, please take me off distribution for these emails."
- "Ralph, I appreciate the emails you have been sending me about this issue. It looks like you have the situation under control so you don't need to send me any more emails unless you have a problem or need my help."
- "It looks like this is an important conversation to have, but I am not sure how I can help. Unless you need action from me, please take me off distribution."
- "If anyone recognizes that I left someone important off this email, please add them and let me know so I can include them in the future."
- "I made some assumptions about who needs to be informed about [state the topic] and put them on the cc line. If I was incorrect, please let me know and I will remove you or add others in future emails."

Key points from Chapter 5

- The principle behind step 3, Addressees, is keep the right people informed. Copy people on emails sparingly only when you have a good answer to the question, "Why is this message useful to someone that has no action?"
- Do not clutter the inboxes of others through the pernicious practice of "reply to all" for things like replies to meeting announcements, feedback to the originator of an email, and questions that pertain only to you.
- If you are not sure whether to copy someone on an email, ask them.
- An Email Ninja focuses communication on just the people that will derive important value from it.
- The acid test for copying someone on email is whether someone is going modify their behavior or change their actions based on your reply.
- Every leader should inform his or her team of what the leader wants to keep informed about.

The next chapter is about the power of composing really brief, descriptive email subjects, with a touch of humor when possible. A really great email subject makes the message content clear *all by itself* and can guide the recipient's attention to focus on your email first out of the many others in their crowded inbox.

Chapter 6-Step 4: Subject as Art

BLUF: Your email subject is the gateway to more effective email communications. Grab the reader's attention by making message content clear from the subject line alone. Brevity, humor, and creative punctuation act like magnets to pull attention to your message in an inbox.

Introduction

An Email Ninja *designs* their email subjects so they stand out to get the action they want when they want it. An Email Ninja doesn't send a meeting agenda with a boring, cryptic subject like "meeting" or "tomorrow". An Email Ninja uses a brief, clear subject that immediately communicates the intent of their message like "Agenda and brief notes for call 25 Sept 8". In this chapter, you will learn how to frame the core idea of your emails into great subjects. Great subject draw reader attention like someone standing on the roadside spinning a brightly colored sign, but your arms won't get as tired and you won't have to dress up like the Statue of Liberty.

Your email *needs* to stand out because it has a lot of competition in reader's inboxes. Your rivals for attention are other high priority messages announcing one-day sales, dating opportunities, corrupted file warnings from services you don't use, and faux shipment notifications about stuff you didn't order. People get a lot of "urgent" emails.

This chapter identifies the email attention challenge we all face, how to overcome texting habits if email is not your "dominant mode," getting positive and avoiding negative attention with email subjects, my highly speculative and imaginative theory to explain why so many people choose really boring subjects, communications principles behind creating imaginative, eye-catching subjects, using punctuation and humor to make your email subjects sparkle, and a five-step process for creating great subject using the acronym PIKER. You will get many practice opportunities throughout the chapter to enact the principles and to make the email subject design process stick. Read on to learn how to make catchy email subject design part of the way you communicate.

Email Subjects are Really Important

The principle behind step 4 of the PAASTUB process, Subject as Art, is make the message content clear from the subject alone. The subject of your email needs to be eye-catching and compelling. Think of the subject of your email as a sparkling, shiny introduction to your message. Spammers and scammers have figured this out because getting their next meal *depends* on getting you to open their email.

Modern, portable, screen-based electronic communications are a mixed blessing. The wonderful thing is you can connect with other people no matter where you are or what time it is for them. The bad thing is that salespeople, scammers, the unskilled, and algorithms *that never sleep* can do the same thing. People get bombarded with automatic emails and text messages informing them of how many social media updates they "missed," who endorsed them, sales and new products from businesses they have connected with, how many more reviews they need to do to earn a reward, who has searched for them or looked at their profile, and all the cat videos posted in the last thirty seconds. The attention carpet bombing practiced by social media platforms and sales algorithms "works." Their paychecks depend on it.

No company today is satisfied with merely selling their product or service to you. They are in an arms race with every other modern business for a bigger and bigger share of your scarce attention. They inundate social media, pester you to "like" them, and distract you with pop up screens on their websites that can't be dismissed until you agree to sign up for the weekly email newsletter you already receive! They send email to inform you about sales every fifteen minutes, provide tips about using their software, or ask you to complete lengthy surveys ("your opinion matters!"). Note the energy and urgency conveyed by the subjects of just a few of the marketing messages from my spam folder:

- Ends Today:
- 50% off sale ends tomorrow
- Don't be left out! Sale starts NOW
- Event X is coming: Get Ready!
- What's the Secret to Team Success?
- Reveal your bonus offer before its too late
- (FINAL REMINDER)
- [Action Required] ...

- Last Chance
- YOUR PAYMENT CONFIRMATION
- Exclusive. Premium …
- rtsoule: Call 123-555-7890

These subjects give you the feeling like all life will stop instantaneously and every molecule in your body will explode if you don't open them RIGHT NOW. I have to practice mental relaxation techniques after every time I look at my spam folder.

Busy people only have time to quickly survey their email inboxes during really short breaks between meetings, phone calls, and urgent issues. Unless you're the boss, your message has to compete for attention with a complicated mess of urgent-looking marketing, training, and funeral announcements. Emails with less interesting, non-urgent, or vague subjects like "meeting" get skipped, mentally filed in the "when I have time" category. As new bake sale emails arrive, messages that were bypassed on earlier scans may scroll so far down in a person's inbox that they aren't visible in the first screenful. Uh oh.

Sending and reading emails with great subjects at work can be a new concept for experienced as well as new members of the workforce. Most experienced senders of email have never had any training about the importance of designing artful subjects. If they had any training it all, it was most likely how the email program works, not how to make it work for them to get things done. Many new entrants to the workforce, the digital natives, grew up with text messaging. They seldom make phone calls and have texted since they were old enough to hold a cell phone. For these workers, sending emails is something their parents did, but not them. Grasping the leverage of Step 4, Subject as Art, can is a leap for them because text messages don't have subjects. Their first question is, "What's a subject?" Text and chat don't need subjects because the communication is so brief and focused on "in the moment" issues.

Why Poor Subjects Are So Common

Why is your inbox filled with boring, vague email subjects (except for spam)? There are several factors that contribute to making make poor email subjects the norm. As I noted in Chapter 2, the typical process flow of email leads people to compose the subject before the body of the email. Second, the sender's focus for a new email is on the body of the email, not the subject. Third, the value of a brilliant subject is under-appreciated, possibly because people have so little experience getting emails that have them.

Bad email subject factor one is that users aren't clear about what they are going to write when they begin a new email. The idea frequently starts abstract, usually something like "send an email invitation to members of the team for our next meeting." They accept the need to put something in the subject blank before they compose the email as a given. My experience suggests that most people aren't ready to provide a good subject before they write the email. This leads directly to factor two.

Bad email subject factor two is that facing a blank subject field at the beginning of the composition flow of email programs can lead to dysfunctional mental shortcuts. We tend to have a positive mental image of shortcuts. Most of the time, shortcuts are good because they are efficient. They save us time and work. We get to our destination faster. Unfortunately, an email subject that is quick, easy, and mentally efficient for you (like "meeting") is detrimental to getting your email "noticed" in someone's inbox.

Bad email subject factor three is that clarity about the contents of the email only comes after you compose it. You may think you know, but you can't be sure until you see what you wrote. What you want to communicate often changes several times as you write the message. Actions and deadlines have a way of sneaking into emails as you write them. This is a natural part of the writing process, but it is deadly for creating email subjects with clarity, brevity, and focus.

Bad email subject factor four is most people don't realize how high-leverage a really good (with clarity, brevity, and focus) email subject is. They just don't give much thought to the subject of their email. When I teach people how to create clarity, brevity, and focus in email subjects, they are invariably astonished at what it does for the response rate of their emails. The importance and value of brilliant email subjects never occurred to them. The importance of the email subject is never addressed in any email training so it seldom occurs to people.

The informal, short bursts of text common to chat and instant messaging can lead to communications disabilities that need to be overcome. These disabilities are major obstacles to communicating effectively with email and they are not confined to just inveterate texters. The first disability is thinking that email is all about you. Not at all. Professional email is about getting work done. It has to focus on your readers and what they need to give you what you need. Your readers need a clear, brief, compelling reason to open your message: your email subject. With all the stuff that gets dropped into inboxes, your subject is the only leverage you have in the competition for your readers' attention. It's what this chapter is about.

The second disability is not packaging everything the reader needs to get something done. Unlike chat, emails are not an invitation to a lively back and forth exchange that may or may not be focused on accomplishing anything. Emails need to express a complete idea, like preparation for a meeting, and provide all resources for action in a single message. I address the first disability in this chapter and the second in   Chapter 4 Action, Chapter 9 BLUF-ing, Chapter 10 Strategies for Specific Kinds of Emails, and Chapter 11 Tactics for High Leverage. Overcoming the second disability has many elements, which is why it requires multiple chapters.

Key Ideas for Subject Greatness

Are you trapped by the process flow of email, mental shortcuts, clarity at the end of the message, and lack of awareness? Absolutely not. You can tackle these dysfunctional email subject factors head on. You can become part of the solution and not the problem. In the next section, I break down the Key Ideas underlying great email subjects into small, actionable steps, which makes them easier to learn so they become habits faster.

Whether you are new to or familiar with email, think of the subject as the one phrase you are allowed to motivate someone to read your email. A clear, brief, and focused subject is compelling. It is essential for getting attention. The sections of the chapter that follow show you how to create really good subjects that, like spammers and scammers, create the "pull" for your recipients to open your email. After learning the key elements of really good subject, you will have a chance to practice the skills involved so they become second nature.

So how does an Email Ninja achieve clarity with brevity and focus in an email subject? They do it by employing four key ideas:

1.   Embrace the notion that people open and read your email based on the subject alone.

2.   Focus the subject on conveying the content of the message as clearly as possible.

3.   Keep the subject short (really short).

4.   Revisit the subject and compare it several times to what you have written before hitting "send."

These key ideas work together to a forge tight link between the purpose and content of the message and the reader's attention.

First, an Email Ninja accepts that the subject may be the only thing recipients read, at least at first. Unless your subject is compelling, a busy person won't open it. People only have so much attention they can devote to email. Most recipients quickly scan the email subjects in their inboxes as they decide "what's next?" Really. An Email Ninja embraces this challenge.

Second, an Email Ninja makes the content of the message clear **from the subject alone**. Their subject alerts readers to action they want, help they need, or information they are providing. For a really short communication, they can get their point across with just a subject and no message body, almost like a text message. For example, to cancel a meeting, a subject like "Must canx call-have guests-will resked" is sufficient with no message.

Third, an Email Ninja puts their subject on a tight budget. Really tight, like the Grinch's shoes or Scrooge's wallet. 25-30 characters is the optimal length of an email subject because some people read most of their email on mobile devices with tiny screens. Abbreviate ruthlessly: write "8a" instead of "8:00 am," "fbk" instead of "feedback," "ltr" instead of "letter," and "mtg" instead of "meeting." It is a good practice to use abbreviations that will be recognizable to recipients, but be willing to push the envelope slightly. I use "pptx" instead of "Power Point file" and no one has ever been confused. What is most important about this Key Idea is not the actual subject character count, but keeping it brief and focused. It's "just the facts, Ma'am."

Fourth, an Email Ninja always rethinks the subject after composing the email. This is when they have the greatest clarity on the type of email: action, information, a request for help, meeting set up, or reporting a problem. It is also when they are clearest on due dates. They accept this reality, embrace it, and get on with thinking carefully about their subject after they have written the email.

As an example of the four key ideas in action, imagine that you have a fool-proof plan for ending world hunger in just 30 days. You'd want to share your plan with the senior leaders of your organization, right? This is a sure-fire path to fortune and glory if you can get them to read your email (Key Idea 1). Before you compose the email that will start you down the path to fortune and glory, your first subject drafts might be things like "world hunger", "plan", or "great idea". After writing the email describing your plan, you realize that none of those initial subjects make it clear what the email is about (Key Idea 2) so you revisit your original subject (Key Idea 4). The revision of your subject is "I know how to end world hunger and the plan can be implemented in 30 days" (Key Idea 2). If you were riding in an elevator between two closely-spaced floors with a senior leader, that's what you would tell them so you could gage their reaction.

The problem is, you are not in an elevator so you have to compose an email with a compelling subject (clarity, brevity, and focus). Your elevator speech version of the subject was 73 characters. Whoa! This is so long that it is likely to get cut off, which would be bad. Once the subject gets truncated, the email system is in control of what your recipient sees, not you. To get the most important information into the first 25-30 characters of the subject (Key Idea 3), an Email Ninja takes a chainsaw to the original subject! The revisions might look like this:

• Elevator Speech: "I know how to end world hunger and the plan can be implemented in 30 days"- 73 characters

• Version 2: "My really awesome strategy to totally end world hunger in 30 days"- 65 characters

• Version 3: "My plan ends world hunger in 30 days" - 36 characters

• Version 4: "Plan-world hunger ends-30 days"- 30 characters

• Version 5: "Plan-end world hunger-30days" - 28 characters

• Version 6: "Plan ends hunger 30 days" - 24 characters

Version 6 will not sit unread in an inbox as long as version 2, "My really awesome strateg ...", which is how it could get truncated.

An Email Ninja's goal is for all email subjects to have clarity, brevity, and focus. This example illustrates two additional points about the application of the Key Ideas of creating an artful email subject.

First, you must start with a really clear idea of what your email is about. This will most likely occur after you have composed the message. Second, artful subjects will not jump right out of your brain until you get lots of practice. Embrace the notion that they come through successive edits of the text.

Even Email Ninjas seldom create an artful subject only 30 characters long on the first try. It takes a lot of creativity to balance clear content and brevity. An Email Ninja enjoys the challenge of creating artful email subjects because of the impact they have on the recipient's attention. That is the payoff of applying the four Key Ideas of email subject greatness. The next section describes how using keywords and creative punctuation function as additional tools for great subjects.

Keywords, Punctuation, and Humor

An Email Ninja uses keywords, creative punctuation, and humor to make their subject stand out. These are incredibly useful for creating a brief subject that has clarity and focus. Subject keywords are like road signs: they alert readers to what's coming ahead. Creative punctuation makes text stand out more clearly. A touch of humor or irony in subjects is a third way to get positive attention. I will explain each in turn.

Merriam Webster defines a keyword as "a significant word from a title or document used especially as an index to content." Subject keywords help you to convey understanding faster. They keep email subjects brief and get across important information. An email subject keyword is a short word or two at the beginning of the subject that indicates what the email is about.

For example, instead of using the subject:

"Just for your information, here is a description of frog mating habits" (70 characters)

An Email Ninja would use:
"Info-frog mating habits" (23 characters)

Below is the list of keywords I use most often to get recipient attention. As you read the list, you might think of other keywords that you prefer instead of mine. No problem, adapt this list as necessary to create your own. Just make sure the keywords you use are as short and easy to recognize as mine. In order of message content priority, the keywords are:

- **Alert** (big problem, read right away)
- **HOT** (very important, better than URGENT because it is shorter, but don't overuse)
- **Problem** (but not a big problem). An alternative, more humorous version is "Uh-oh" (see below). Both "problem" and "uh-oh" are better than "PLEASE READ" or "Important" because they are shorter. For big problems, you could use Alert, HOT, or Big Prob.
- **Ouch** (something gone wrong, unexpected or difficult). This is an example of mixing keywords with some humor.
- **Action** (you want the recipient to do something based on the email).   Always include a due date in the subject of an "action" email like "due 1-18: Action-provide comments on plan".
- **Need Help** (a more gentle way to request action). Use with superiors or people you don't know well.
- **Question** (makes it clear you need something, more compelling and thus likely to get opened faster than "Re: (the old subject)"). I sometimes use "Confused" as an attention grabber.
- **No fwd** (for sending sensitive emails that requires special handling). "No fwd" is not a free pass to write disparaging things about others. Always explain why you don't want the message forwarded in the first few characters of the email.
- **Update** (new information, more compelling than "Re: the boring old subject")
- **Reminder** (when you have sent one email already, but received no response). Be gentle and polite when sending reminder emails to avoid really annoying the receiver and getting put into "ignore" mode.
- **Mtg** (for meeting details, include topic, date, time, location right in the subject). Call or Event are good alternatives such as "Call: 28 Jan 1p-Episode 30 recording"
- Info (no action, recipients should open only they have time or **interest**)
- Late (lets people know you are late responding)
- Long or **Long msg** (warns readers that it will take some time to read the message you are sending)

Here are five quick tips for using keywords and making them more effective.

- First, always put them at the beginning of the subject so they won't be truncated.
- Second, the keyword should replace "fw" or "re" at the beginning of emails. Fw and re are like keywords, but their information content is really low. They don't say much about message content so the "fw" and "re" text serve no purpose when you use a subject keyword.
- Third, don't be too creative with your keywords. Like roadway signs, they need to be instantly recognizable. If an Email Ninja thinks a recipient might not be familiar with a keyword, they will explain it briefly at the top of the message. At the bottom of the message, they will include a short list of the keywords they use frequently and how they define them. Keeping the list in a draft email message is a quick way to have it readily available.
- Fourth, don't overuse the high priority keywords. If everything you send is "hot", you have issues prioritizing your work that Email Ninja skills won't fix.
- Fifth, consider using a keyword for all emails related to a specific project or event. For example, if you are working on a project to end world hunger, project team members could begin email subjects for messages related to the project with "End Hunger-". Just make sure that everyone knows this and gently correct people when they forget by changing their subject when you reply.

Keywords that I never use are "Save the Date" and "Please Read". "Save the Date" is too long. "Mtg" or "Event" are clearer and briefer. The people that do use "Save the Date" frequently err by not including event details in the subject, which forces recipients to open the email to figure out why they should be saving some future, unspecified date.

Compare this subject:

"Save the date: Bob's retirement party" (36 characters)

with the subject an Email Ninja would use:

"Event-Bob retires party 12 May 4p" (33 characters)

If an Email Ninja needed RSVPs for the party invitations, they would use:

"RSVP-Bob retires party 12 May 4p"

The "Save the date" subject tells the reader nothing other than Bob is retiring. In the second case, the reader knows, from the subject alone, that Bob is retiring and when the party occurs. Not only is the second subject shorter, but it contains all the essential scheduling information so recipients can check their calendars without having to open the message! "Bob retires party" is a bit more awkward than "Bob's retirement party," but it's better because it is shorter.

As a keyword, "Please Read" is artless and practically useless. What makes an email with this keyword special? Does this keyword give recipients permission to delete other emails from the sender without reading? I think other keywords are more useful. "Problem" indicates the sender is trying to communicate something really important and implies there may be action for the recipient. If there is no problem, but you need the recipient to do something, use the keyword "Action" or "Need help", which won't sit in anyone's email inbox unopened for long.

A final thought on keywords: remove them when they no longer apply. Once you have recipients' attention for a really important issue, the keyword "Hot" serves no useful purpose so remove it for future back and forth communications. I have seen URGENT remain in email subjects long after the contents are no longer urgent, which defeats the purpose of using it as a keyword. It also risks distracting busy people when communications de-escalate from high priority to routine.

Creative use of punctuation can really help keep the subject brief and get the recipient's attention. The function of normal punctuation is to organize the way words are arranged to improve readability and understanding. In email subjects, you can use dashes or parentheses differently than you normally would. They can split ideas apart to convey different meanings or add crispness and clarity. Here's how:

Get extra focus on important text like due dates. Instead of:

"Need help by 30 Jan for letter of recommendation" (49 characters) an Email Ninja would use:

(Due 30 Jan)-Need ltr of rec" (28 characters). Isolating the due date with parentheses makes it stand out better. The dash splits the date from what is due.

Don't use colons (":") in subjects because they need a space afterward to make them visible. An Email Ninja uses a single dash ("-") instead. Saving a single character in email subjects is not trivial. Every space counts in the battle for reader attention.

Instead of:

"Save the date: world ends tomorrow" (34 characters)

An Email Ninja would use:

"Alert-world ends tomorrow" (25 characters)

Humorous and imaginative subjects, when appropriate, are particularly good ways to get recipients to open your emails first. Crafting appropriate email subjects is a wonderful opportunity to display creativity and playfulness that make your messages stand out. Humor, playfulness, and irony are unusual in email subjects and act like magnets for attention to get your emails opened faster. Receivers probably don't get much humor in their inbox so a certain amount of "goofiness" on your part may come across as "adorkable" in a way that is both appealing and sparks interest in opening the message sooner. Humorous or playful keywords and subjects that an Email Ninja might use include:

- Uh-oh (something unexpected), "Uh-oh, Ralph's account deactivated" (34 characters)
- Darn (indicates an error in a previous email or inability to attend an event), "Darn-file now attached" (22 characters)
- Oops (another way to telegraph an error), "Oops-corrected link" (19 characters)
- Missed the memo (still another way to indicate an error in a previous email or action), "Missed the memo-Ralph's bio attached" (36 characters)

- Bummer (reply to someone that sent bad news), "Bummer-job offer fell through" (29 characters)
- Yay or Good News, "Yay-wife discharged from hosp" (29 characters)

These are are examples from actual emails that I have sent. Use your own sense of humor and creativity to show some style in email subjects. Just stay professional and don't veer into cryptic or rude subjects.

Subject keywords, creative punctuation, and humor all contribute to getting positive attention for your emails that help you cut through the clutter in email inboxes. They just look more interesting. Keywords are repeatable, easily recognizable signs that telegraph the content of your email. Creative punctuation such as enclosing due dates in parentheses or using dashes to separate ideas is helpful for conveying rich meaning in just a few characters. Finally, look for opportunities to use humor and irony in email subjects, especially when you can poke fun at yourself or a situation. The subject "Bonehead-forgot attachment" is a lot more fun to write too. The next section puts together all the strategies for brilliant subjects into a memorable process flow that will help you become an Email Ninja faster.

Five Steps for Great Subjects

To make your transition from bland subject creator to Email Ninja easier, I have broken down the process of creating brief, artful subjects into five steps. The five steps are designed to produce a more effective process flow for great subjects, subjects that have clarity, brevity, and focus. The five steps use the acronym **PIKER** to make them easier to remember. The **PIKER** steps are:

- **Preliminary** subject. With your purpose firmly in mind, start composing your email by describing that purpose. Write just one phrase for what the email message says or is about. You might revise the subject at least once to get it shorter, but don't get hung up on this step. Move on quickly to the next one.
- **Inscribe** (write) your email. Your purpose will become clearer as you write. Don't ramble. Be clear about the "action" (what you want and when) in the first two sentences.
- **Keyword** selection. With your email message written, come back

to the subject. Choose a keyword, if appropriate, that describes the kind of message it is. Keywords aren't essential, but choosing a keyword makes you think again about how to manage the recipient's focus.

- **Edit** the subject. Once you have written the email, your purpose is much clearer than when you chose a preliminary subject. Now try to reduce the subject to 25-30 characters. Creative punctuation and abbreviations help a lot. Consider whether you can make the subject funny or ironic.

- **Re-check** the subject. Do this several times. This might sound hard, but it isn't after you do it a few times. As you review the subject, ask yourself, "Does my *subject alone* tell the reader what they need to know about my email?" This is a very high standard for email subject quality, but it makes an enormous difference in email effectiveness. An Email Ninja strives to meet the standard with every email.

The next section gives you opportunities to practice writing email subjects with clarity, brevity, and focus. Writing great email subjects is like any other skill, it is improved through practice.

Practice

Compose email subjects for the BLUFs below. Keep the subjects short and remember to use keywords, if you can. My suggested subjects are on [the next page]. The point of the exercise is not to match the answer I provided, but to practice creating subjects with clarity, brevity, and focus to *pull* recipients toward opening your emails faster.

BLUF 1: By 6th of MAY: Please indicate if you think we ought to apply for this funding stream from X to organize an event for PhD's and early career researchers.

BLUF 2: Here is a brief introduction to me and the kind of research I would like to do. I want your feedback on what I have written so far.

BLUF 3: Let's do the call Monday at 10:00 am. I will call you.

BLUF 4: Invitations have been sent for the call Sunday, 10a MDST, 12p EDST, 5p BST. Here is the agenda based on previous inputs with a few small edits.

BLUF 5: I would like to get your perspective and possibly some advice on my post-doctoral degree plans.

BLUF 6: Read ahead for call scheduled 9 Nov, 8am - 9 am.

BLUF 7: You might want to look into this program. It is a word processor for audio files. It is only available for Macs at present. I have downloaded a copy and signed up for the transcription service. Below is a link to the FAQ.

BLUF 8: I want to replace the wallet that arrived today, order number 2273. It has a very large scratch on one side. How do I do this?

BLUF 9: Please review my storyboard and the pptx based on it. Let me know what it makes *you* think of as you read it.

BLUF 10: Please review and comment by 12 Mar on my one-page summary of a proposed research project, if you have time.

BLUF 11: Please consider providing a reference letter by 6 Mar. I am applying for a position that requires reference letters in advance. I will gather the job description details and everything I submitted and provide it to you along with areas to emphasize.

Answers to Practice Subjects

BLUF 1: By 6th of MAY: Please indicate if you think we ought to apply for this funding stream from X to organize an event for PhD's and early career researchers.
Subject: Due 6 May-apply for event funding? (34 characters)

BLUF 2: Here is a brief introduction to me and the kind of research I would like to do. I want your feedback on what I have written so far.
Subject: Seeking fbk-Soule intro for research (36 characters)

BLUF 3: Let's do the call Monday at 10:00. I will call you.
Subject: Talk Mon 10a-Ralph calls (24 characters)

BLUF 4: -Invitations have been sent for the call Sunday, 10a MDST, 12p EDST, 5p BST. Here is the agenda based on previous inputs with a few small edits.
Subject: Agenda, notes for review mtg Sun (32 characters). Note: I did not put the times in the subject because there were too many time zones involved

BLUF 5: I would like to get your perspective and possibly some advice on my post-doctoral degree plans.
Subject: Prep info for advice call (25 characters)

BLUF 6: Read ahead for call scheduled 9 Nov, 8am - 9 am.
Subject: Read ahead-call Mon, Nov 9, 8-9a (32 characters)

BLUF 7: You might want to look into this program that is a word processor for audio files. It is only available for Macs at present. I have downloaded a copy and signed up for the transcription service. Below is a link to the FAQ.
Subject: Useful? Word processor for audio

BLUF 8: I want to replace the wallet that arrived today, order number 2273. It has a very large scratch on one side. How do I do this?
Subject: Problem-wallet scratched, order 2273 (36 characters)

BLUF 9: Please review my storyboard and the pptx based on it. Let me know what it makes *you* think of as you read it.

Subject: (what was he thinking?)-My Storyboard (37 characters)

BLUF 10: Please review and comment by 12 Mar on my one-page summary of a proposed research project, if you have time.
    Subject: Pls review 12 Mar: one-page on heritage museum (46 characters)

BLUF 11: Please consider providing a reference letter by 6 Mar. I came across a position that I think I would really enjoy that requires reference letters in advance. I will gather the job description details and everything I submitted and provide it to you along with areas to emphasize.
    Subject: (due 3/6/17)Ref Ltr Req-job app (31 characters)

Key points from Chapter 6

- You need clarity, brevity, and focus in every email subject you write.
- A well-designed email subject can pull the receiver's attention to your email like a magnet.
- The purpose of your email subject should be to make the answer to "what does this mean to me?" *instantly* clear to recipients.
- Keep your subject clear, but as short as possible so it won't get shortened by the email system.
- Your email subject should be a sparkling introduction *inviting* readers to open your message.
- Use keywords like Hot, Problem, and Ouch as traffic signs to signal what's ahead in your message.
- Don't waste subject characters on vague, meaningless text like "save the date."
- Humorous or ironic subjects make your email more compelling.
- Don't reuse old email subjects when the topic has changed, especially if they contain words like "urgent."
- When you add new text to email subjects, put it at the beginning to keep it from getting shortened.

The next chapter spotlights the need to take the "trash" out of emails. This makes them shorter, enabling recipients to scan them quickly for the information they need, which helps them take action faster.

Chapter 7-Step 5: Take Out the Trash

BLUF: "Take out the trash" from emails means to remove all unnecessary text before you send them. Reduce the text to focus readers on just what is important for accomplishing your purpose. It takes time for you to remove extraneous text, but readers will appreciate your email clarity and succinctness.

Introduction

Email is a wonderful tool because it allows for asynchronous communication over extended periods. However, multiple emails back and forth between groups of people can be like a tumbleweed blowing across the desert, picking up all sorts of debris: multiple copies of the same, tiresome and long email signatures; forwards with no new information; personal messages; and information that is out of date. After just a few forwards and replies, only a fraction of the text of most emails remains relevant to readers. You should take out the trash, my term for any text from other people that does not contribute to your message. This is important because it can take a lot of recipient mental energy to tune out the noise in long email threads.

You want readers to focus on providing just what *you* need. Step 5 of the PAASTUB process, Take Out the Trash, is designed to get this focus. This chapter provides examples of what I consider superfluous email text, warnings of what can happen when you don't remove this trash, and some thoughts about the balance necessary between editing with zeal and providing sufficient context.

Make Your Messages Easy to Scan

The principle behind step 5, Take Out the Trash, is remove all unnecessary text from email to make messages easy to scan. This lets readers focus on the most important information for your purpose. It means eliminating everything that does not directly support the purpose of your email.

If you are composing a new email message, start with the action or main idea and only include what recipients need to understand what you want, its importance, and when you need it. For information emails, clearly and succinctly state how you expect the recipient to benefit from what you are providing. If you are replying to or forwarding an email message, remove all the unnecessary text from others that might distract readers or make the message hard to read quickly.

When I open an email, I want to know what I need to do with it. I scan the text quickly looking for answers to five questions.

1. What is this?
2. How is it relevant to me?
3. What is the action?
4. When is the action needed, now or later?
5. If there is no action right away, where should I put this so I can get back to it later?

Your email message should communicate succinct answers to the first four questions: what, relevance, action, and when action is needed. The fifth question is up to the reader entirely.

What do I mean by "trash"? I consider email trash to be anything in an email that gets between the recipient and answering the first four processing questions above:

1. what,
2. relevance,
3. action, and
4. when action is needed.

Here are some examples of what I consider trash in email: verbose signatures with quotes from famous people, multiple copies of the same email signature, disclaimers and privacy notices that threaten me with grievous bodily and legal harm if I read something not meant for my eyes, repeat addressees from prior emails, message headers (time, date, poor subjects, "original message" text) from previous replies and forwards, and text that is no longer relevant. I will explain each form of trash in turn.

- Long signatures. Email signatures that go beyond name, email address, and phone number are just a lot of extra text for recipients to wade through. If recipients want to know your job title, office code, address, zodiac sign, favorite superhero, and shoe size, they will ask. Including a quote that you find inspirational is also unnecessary. Most recipients really don't care about your favorite philosophies and aphorisms. As I discuss in more detail in Chapter 11, the Shorten Signatures section, consider simplifying your email signature to just name, address, and phone number.

- Multiple copies of email signatures. When you reply to or forward an email that already has replies from many other people, the number of repetitive email signatures grows rapidly. When your recipients need to read input from others in previous forwards and replies, they only need to see ONE copy of each unique signature. Leave just one, brief signature per person in the body of the email. Having a person's title, email address, and phone numbers might be useful, but not ten copies of it. If you reply more than once to an email thread, don't contribute to the problem of repetitive signatures. Only include your signature once.

- Disclaimers. I could probably write a whole chapter about this irritating text of dubious value that some organizations require on all emails. Sadly, it would be a waste of time so I won't. If your organization requires these, fine. They probably won't distract email recipients at the bottom of an email because few people will bother to read them. Disclaimers and privacy warnings from others scattered throughout a long series of replies and forward can be very distracting. You should eliminate them from any email message you send. I doubt you will get a visit from the disclaimer police for doing so.

- Message headers. Many email programs copy the header as well as the text of the previous email message on replies and forwards. The header may include text like "original email", the time and date an email was sent, recipients, and the subject. There are very few instances where any of this text adds value to what you want to send. In rare circumstances, it is useful for your recipients to know when senior people were part of the earlier email distribution. I recommend deleting all the header information from previous email messages except the sender and the date sent.

- Text that is no longer relevant. Email threads consisting of a long series of replies and forwards inevitably contain text that adds no value. Examples are mere forwards and "FYIs" that have no body text, only brief questions, and salutations like "Dear Ralph" and other personal messages. Even though email is informal and probably does not *need* text like "Dear Ralph" and a few lines inquiring about his family, I recognize that some people want to include it because it makes the email message feel more personal. Multiple emails later when I am replying to or forwarding the message to someone else, it no longer adds any value to *my* email. Whenever I remove text from the body of a prior email, I use ellipsis marks "…" to clearly indicate that I have removed text. If I think it is useful to paraphrase what someone wrote previously to express it more clearly, I put the replacement text in [brakets].

Since it takes time and some judgment to take out the trash from prior email messages, why bother? First, very few people take the time to do it. Removing unnecessary text makes the brevity and clarity of your emails really stand out. You may not get feedback about this at first, but people will notice. Second, it is hard for readers to quickly scan emails that have lots of text that is a mix of useful and useless information. Readers want to know: what was the original issue, what did others contribute, has the issue or how people understand it changed, is there action, or do people need more information? When you spare readers this effort, you simplify their mental effort so they can focus on what's important, *which you decided* before you sent the email. Mental effort is scarcer than fossil fuels in many business environments.

Messy email text has negative real-world consequences. Several years ago, NASA and the French space agency were coordinating a joint mission. NASA personnel became frustrated with how long it took the French to respond to email requests for action. What NASA personnel didn't know was that it sometimes took three days for the recipients of the email to translate all the technical information embedded in the replies and forwards that were left in the message below the action requests. The French recipients wanted to make sure they understood the context of the message before replying. NASA personnel might have sped things up considerably if they had made sure their emails only contained the most relevant and important information related to their action requests.

Sometimes, taking out the trash is more than just eliminating irrelevant text. When you add someone new to a long string of email messages, you should add a sentence or two that summarizes the previous communications: what the problem is and the various concerns or positions of others. I use text like "For Bob: this is why I included you and this what has been discussed to date." Many times, I was added to an email discussion and had no idea why.

The difficult issue with respect to taking out the trash from email you send is how much do you delete? The simple answer is "As much as you can, but not more than your recipients need." The questions you need to ask yourself while taking out the trash are: How much of context is necessary for your recipients to understand and what is the best way to give it to them? Is it better to include large amounts of original text or a few short sentences summarizing it, or both? Sometimes I provide a brief summary of the contributions of other people before the original email text (not my reply) and include lightly edited text below that. In this way, readers can see what I thought was important and read further if they have questions.

The amount of context you include to support the action you want is a decision only you can make. Regardless of your decision, the best way to provide context for your message recipients is to filter, summarize, and simplify the replies and forwards that occurred prior to composing your email message.

An Email Ninja strives to make it easy for the recipients to read their emails and quickly understand the issue and action. If you are adding someone new to an ongoing discussion, make it easy for them to understand what has come before your email message. Since you have already done the mental heavy lifting to understand what is important in the email you are passing along, take advantage of your effort. This is easy for you and much harder for others. Take the trash out of email messages and only including text that addresses what the message is about, its relevance, and when action is needed.

Examples of text to remove from emails that you forward

- Multiple copies of the same, lengthy email signature (yours or others', this includes any text after the final paragraph of a message)
- All copies of email disclaimers and privacy warnings (usually found at the bottom of emails)
- All salutations ("Dear ...") and closings ("Best," "Best Regards," etc.)
- Lists of recipients of prior emails (almost never relevant)
- All prior email subjects (not relevant to what you are trying to communicate)

Key points from Chapter 7

- The principle behind step 5, Take Out the Trash, is focus on the most important information for your purpose by removing unnecessary text.
- Focusing on the reader and don't leave it to them to figure out what is important and what isn't in the emails you send.
- Examples of trash to take out of your emails: multiple or long email signatures, quotes from famous people, disclaimers and privacy warnings, repetitive addressees and message headers from prior emails, and text that is no longer relevant.
- Reduce the email mental burden on your recipients by making it easy for them to read your email and quickly understand the issue and action. Include just enough of the original text of prior emails to do this.
- When you add someone new to a series of replies and forwards, explain at the top of the message why you added them and summarize the previous messages.

The next chapter focuses on editing the "ugly remarks" from emails to make your emails more professional and avoid pain and embarrassment. Venting your emotions or including them from prior emails is not a strategy for personal success.

Chapter 8-Step 6: Ugly Remarks Edited

BLUF: Delete or paraphrase ugly (insensitive or intemperate) remarks in email from yourself or others to avoid future pain and embarrassment. Send a separate note to people that write such things asking them refrain in the future.

Introduction

One of the most important guidelines of email etiquette is don't strongly criticize or write harsh things about others. This is important because strong emotions and harsh language or criticism reflect poorly on you and your communications skills. Step 6 of the PAASTUB process, Ugly Remarks Edited, focuses your attention on this truism to keep sensitive or potentially upsetting verbiage out of your emails. This chapter identifies the principle behind Step 6, why strong emotions have no place in professional, effective communications, reasons why you should keep ugly remarks out of your emails, examples of ugly remarks, rules of thumb for identifying negative statements as you compose your emails, and two techniques for keeping negative statements out of emails you write or forward. Step 6, Ugly Remarks Edited, is designed to make you more aware of the dangers of harsh language and criticism so you can avoid the damage they can cause to relationships and your professional reputation.

Stay Out of Trouble

The principle behind step 6, Ugly Remarks Edited, is keep yourself and others out of trouble by removing angry or rash text. Writing or including sensitive comments from others in email messages just creates fodder for juicy wiki-leaks stories that won't reflect well on you. In fact, personal observations on what you or others perceive to be the shortcomings of others make you appear small minded and petty.

There is a great deal of scientific research suggesting that you don't reason well when you are upset or angry. When you are upset with someone, the last thing you should do is write him or her an e-mail message to get things off your chest. When you are experiencing strong emotions, your normal defenses are not as effective against using making disparaging remarks that might upset others. While it is perfectly normal to get frustrated or upset, keep it to yourself or confine it to a small social circle and verbal communications only. Email messages leave long-lasting records that can complicate or damage professional and personal relationships, sometimes permanently.

Never send email when you are upset or angry. While there is value in the emotional release provided by getting things "off your chest," DON'T PUT IT IN EMAIL. If you have written an email with some strongly worded criticism or an angry response, don't hit "send." Just save it to drafts so you can review it later when you are calmer, less upset, and more likely to delete it than send it. Email is not an effective communications method when strong emotions are involved unless you want people to know how immature and petty you can be.

Avoid making negative statements about other people or organizations in email messages. This includes criticism directed at the recipient or others not on the email distribution. This is important for several reasons. First, criticism typically comes across much harsher in text form than when delivered face-to-face. Criticism in email lacks important, non-verbal social cues for communication such as body language, facial expressions, tone of voice, and other signals that are important elements of face-to-face communications. Second, the value of "speaking your mind" or telling people "what you really think" is vastly overrated. While everyone has personal opinions, exposing them publicly and in the semi-permanent form of email can make you look petty and unprofessional. Third, your negative views of others may be based on incomplete or incorrect data. This is another way of saying "you might be the idiot, not them." Fourth, and most importantly, the chances that the objects of your negative attention will eventually see what you wrote is a lot higher than you might think. Once you send the email message, you have NO CONTROL of what others do with it and where they send it. None. You have no idea how many or few degrees of separation exist between you and others outside of your personal and professional networks. As an aid to being more cautious against making negative statements about others, I write every email as if I *know* that the people I am writing about will read it.

Negative statements that have no place in email fall into four categories. The first and most obvious type of negative speech is vulgarity or profanity. Regardless of how common it is in internet forums or what it might do for your mental health, it has no place in email, *ever*. The second broad category of negative speech is an ad hominem attack, which involves criticizing a person apart from their position or opinion by using insults or epithets, like referring to them as stupid or an idiot even if you know that their SAT scores were really low. My third category of negative speech is libelous, sexist or racially discriminating comments. It does not matter and is not an excuse if they are meant to be a joke. My fourth category is criticism or second-guessing of someone's decisions or the performance of members of their organization behind their back. Text in your email message that falls under any of these categories is likely to cause problems for you later so don't write this way.

If you feel that you really must communicate something negative or sensitive to someone, stop writing the email and use the phone. Do not use email to discuss business sensitive information with members outside your organization. Your organization will doubtless have detailed policies for what counts as business sensitive information that has to be guarded. If you don't want your email to be quoted in a newspaper account, don't send it.

I have two rules of thumb for identifying negative comments in email messages. First, use the national visibility test. If you would be really embarrassed to have what you write exposed by hackers, printed in an article in a national newspaper, or go viral on the internet, don't write it. If you have already written something and start having second thoughts while reviewing your message, delete or edit it. Reading over your message several times before sending is a good way to catch both errors and text that could be misinterpreted by others. The essence of this test is trying to imagine what others would think about *you* based on what you have written. The second rule of thumb: if you think the person or any member of the organization you are writing about would be troubled or upset by reading what you have just written, change the text. Note that the "truth" value of the text is less relevant than how others might feel about seeing it written.

I have two techniques that are particularly helpful for keeping negative or sensitive comments about others out of my email. First, I imagine the person I am writing about standing next to me listening to me read my email text aloud and try to anticipate their reaction. Second, I actually add the person I am writing about or members of the particular organization to the email message distribution so I *know* they will be informed of what I am writing. That forces me to take greater responsibility for my writing and be much more careful about what I write. These techniques are practically foolproof ways to stay out of trouble unless you have troubles with empathy. If you score consistently low on ability to empathize with others, then show your email to someone you trust to get their reaction before you send it.

An Email Ninja has a duty to modify sensitive verbiage anywhere it appears in an email, regardless of its source. Once he or she sends an email, an Email Ninja takes full responsibility for everything in it, not just what he or she wrote. I use two approaches to modify negative comments made by others. The first is to tone down emotions and negativity by softening it to make it less harsh. The second is to delete it entirely.

Examples of editing or deleting text:

- Instead of "they completely fouled that up," write "this made things very difficult" or "it was problematic" or "many difficulties ensued."
- Instead of writing he or she "is an idiot" or "is incompetent," delete the text completely. Don't bother to paraphrase it. This kind of ad hominem attack has no place in any kind of email even if it is true.
- Instead of writing that the regulator "will never approve this" or "won't let us do this," write that the regulator "may have concerns we need to address."
- Instead of writing that someone "was just trying to [do X],"

delete the text. Are you a mind reader? How do you know what someone was thinking?

- Instead of writing, "this hurt John's feelings," delete the text. It is not your place to speak for John's feelings. That's John's job and he shouldn't do it in email away.

Notice that the language in the examples is less direct and dilutes the point, which is exactly its purpose. Do you really think you are going to make some difficult, upsetting or confusing situation better by writing an email about it? Think about it. Now think *harder*. If you want someone to accept responsibility for poor performance and take action to improve it, you are not likely to get those results from an email. This is especially true if they feel their actions were justified. **If you have any doubt about whether someone will find your email upsetting, don't send it until you have edited the text.**

If I have modified someone else's negative or critical text, I always send a brief email to the author of the negative text gently explaining, without criticizing, why their text was edited or removed. This achieves one important outcome and may accomplish another. First, the email informs the responsible party about my standards, which is always a good thing. Second, it often causes them to reflect on what they wrote and makes them more sensitive to using strong, negative language in email in the future.

There is no doubt that step 6, Ugly Remarks Edited, is extra work. It takes mental effort to imagine how others will react to your email. You may have to read some sections multiple times. It takes time to write an email to someone after you have edited their comments. How can you afford to spend all this extra time on email? This is the wrong question to ask. What you really have to ask yourself is: How can you *not* invest the time given the risk negative email comments present to your reputation? The next section of this chapter gives you the opportunity identify and edit some ugly remarks.

Practice

Make edits to the example emails below to accomplish Ugly Remarks Edited to keep yourself and others out of trouble.

Practice 1

Original text: The leaders in that organization don't know how to set priorities, which is confusing their personnel. They need to get their act together before we can even think about partnering with them on this project.

Edited text: The leaders in that organization are facing many challenges choosing the most important things to work on. We may not be able to partner with them on this project until they decide where they want to focus their resources.

Practice 2

Original text: I don't think they have any idea whatsoever about how to improve safety.

Edited text: Their definition of what constitutes safety may differ from ours. The first thing we need to do is get a common understanding of where the leverage exists to improve safety.

Practice 3

Original text: The main barriers to improvement in our organization are grossly insufficient staff salaries and being forced to comply with idiotic requirements. The ghouls at headquarters are essentially requiring people to work like slaves and doing nothing to reduce the ridiculous rules they have to follow.

Edited Text: A barrier to improving performance is staff compensation and work practices that are difficult to manage. It will be challenging to improve further until these are considered in more detail.

Practice 4

Original text: Mr. Randall completely fails to establish the need for solving his company's problem. We should use this opportunity to put him out of business. He is the source of real damage to our project. There is no organization in this sector more greedy and rapacious than his.

Edited Text: I would like to see more details about the problem Mr. Randall's company is having. It is difficult to analyze his recommendations without more data.

Practice 5

Original text: This project is a disaster. It is a travesty that those who are responsible for the mess are doing nothing to fix it.

Edited Text: The project is currently experiencing considerable difficult. It is important to keep those in headquarters appraised of our challenges so they can provide help.

Some readers might argue, "Hey, you completely changed what the author of the original text said." This is correct, of course. The issue is that ugly, angry, intemperate remarks have no place in email. The edits drain the emotion and vitriol from the text, but retain the basic idea. This prevents the author of those remarks from getting his or her head ripped off.

Key points from Chapter 8

- Never send an email you wrote when you were upset or angry.
- Avoid making or including intemperate statements in email or attachments. Pretend the person or members of the organization you are writing about is reading it. They probably will eventually.
- Copy any person or members of the organization you are writing about.
- Paraphrase or delete text others may find objectionable.
- If you had to modify or delete text from someone else's email before sending yours, follow-up with the person to explain what you did.

The next chapter explains the Bottom Line Up Front (BLUF) of an email, why you need one, and what it should contain.

Chapter 9-Step 7: BLUF-ing

BLUF: The Bottom Line Up Front (BLUF) describes the essence of your email in three sentences, plus or minus one. Reading the BLUF alone should be sufficient to understand both the action and its importance. Creating a good BLUF also helps you clarifies your thoughts about the message.

Introduction

This chapter defines the BLUF, identifies its key elements, and describes how to construct it. BLUF-ing is not about fooling people with your email message, just the opposite. It is about immediately, ruthlessly getting to the point: what you want, why it's important, and when it's needed. Don't beat around the bush or ramble at the beginning of an email. Busy people don't have the attention span or interest. You know who the busy people are in your world because you **never** get email jokes from them.

People accustomed to communicating primarily through text messages, which is just about everyone under the age of 30, are similarly attention-challenged. In the first place, it is hard for them to imagine why anyone would bother sending a message longer than three sentences. In the second place, they have to get back to their social media feeds to see the latest postings of animal videos and pop culture aphorisms.

People are really, really busy in our highly connected, always-on electronic world. Electronic mail ceased being a novelty decades ago. People don't have time to linger over long email message introductions that ramble all over the place.

Focus Attention with the BLUF

The principle behind step 7 is focus attention with a message summary at the beginning of each message. In this section, I begin with my definition of a Bottom Line Up Front (BLUF) and continue with its key elements, explaining what a BLUF is to others, BLUF examples. I conclude with some thoughts about the value of using the BLUF keyword in email messages.

I define the BLUF as: a statement at the top of an email of the issue, the action you want, and when you need it in three, plus or minus one, sentences. A BLUF is like a summary or abstract of the email only much shorter. There is nothing special about "three plus or minus one" for the length of the BLUF, but in my experience anytime your BLUF exceeds four sentences you are rambling. A BLUF is not a Yelp review where a person writes three paragraphs about why they went to dinner, who was with them, the busy day they had, and how long they wanted to go to a particular restaurant *before* writing a SINGLE THING about the food and service. No. The BLUF is "just the facts ma'am" and what you want the reader to remember about the action or information in your email.

Think of your BLUF as the elevator speech for your email. If you stepped into an elevator with one of your recipients and were only traveling a couple of floors, how would you summarize the email?

Try to keep each sentence of the BLUF short, like sound bites or bumper stickers. The ideal BLUF displays completely on a single screen of a smart phone, two at most. You can afford to keep the BLUF so brief because the rest of the email will contain more detail as needed. Abbreviate as much as possible in the BLUF while still keeping the meaning clear.

There are three key elements of the BLUF. The first sentence identifies the issue at hand by answering the question, "What is this about?" In most cases, a single sentence is all you need to answer that question. The second sentence answers the question, "What is the action?" This is what you want the recipients to actually **do** about the issue at hand and when they need to do it. The third sentence answers the question "Why is this important?" Remember, it should be important for the readers as well as you. Otherwise, your email message really belongs on social media, which really is all about you. In rare circumstances, you might need to add a fourth sentence if additional details are necessary to describe the problem or consequences.

If I am going to communicate with someone frequently by email, I invest the time early in our relationship to explain what BLUFs are and why I use them. This pays huge dividends for future communications. I keep a standard explanation of what the BLUF is in my draft email folder just for this purpose. The BLUF is such an intuitive tool to grasp and so powerful that many people will adopt its use right away after you explain it to them.

How do you actually construct a BLUF? For beginners, I break the task of constructing the BLUF into three steps. These small bites will make it easier for you to compose the BLUF and easier for your readers to digest.

Your first sentence needs to be a succinct answer to the question, "What is this about?" For example, "World will end at 10pm without your action" or "I am applying to graduate school and am seeking your recommendation" or "Project funds will be exhausted at the end of this week at current spending level." I have actually used all three of these in the past (even the "world will end" sentence). A mental aid I often use when creating the first sentence of a BLUF is to imagine I am explaining the contents of the email to my wife who does not know anything about the issue. What would I tell her?

The second sentence answers the question, "What action is necessary?" Don't panic. Take a deep breath. You don't need to be gentle or slowly wander toward the action. The BLUF gives you **permission** to be abrupt and you can be as gentle as you want later in the email. When I teach people about the BLUF, I remind them over and over that a BLUF is not rude. I **want** them to get right to the action so I can quickly decide if I can do it. That's not rude; that helps me be more effective. I think this is true for other busy people as well. What you ask for could be a one time action such as "send money now" or it could be a preliminary action such as finding time for a call to discuss future actions. Continuing from the previous examples, the second sentences could be: "Tell me if you can meet before 6pm to review options otherwise I will seek deep shelter" or "Please let me know if you can submit the recommendation by 10 May" or "Please call me today about sending $30M by Friday 4pm."

Note that each of these action sentences are in the form of a standard action statement: who does what by when. If there is action requested, the action sentence of your BLUF should always have these three components. In the case of the graduate school recommendation, the university certainly has some deadline for applications. You should NOT provide that to the person writing the recommendation. You should take the deadline, subtract a week from the date as a safety factor, estimate how long it will take to arrive at the admissions office from the location of the recommender, and give THAT date as the deadline. It is a tenet of project management that you never tell someone the latest possible date they can do anything.

Your third sentence answers the question, "Why is this important?" This is an obligation you have to your recipients otherwise why would you expect them to take the action? Be direct, crisp, and stick to the point. For example, using the previous examples, the third sentence could be: "The enemy has threatened to launch missiles unless we accede to his demands," or "I have attached the necessary form for the university with my personal information" or "Unless you send more money, I have to stop work on this project." The example sentences may seem harsh, but your busy reader will really appreciate this clarity.

You should consider finishing the BLUF with a statement about whether reply to all is appropriate. As the message originator, you are in the best position to know this. As discussed in Chapter 5, Addressees, you can use text like: "Please reply to all" or "Please don't reply to all."

In some cases, the reader(s) of your email will already grasp why the issue is important. They may be so involved with the details of your project or activity that your second sentence just needs to provide further details of the problem. Be careful of providing excessive detail, however.

Some people might think it is rude or too abrupt to begin emails with a BLUF. Perhaps, but getting right to the bottom line of the message reflects a focus on the reader, the fundamental principle of this book. You are actually helping the reader quickly understand what you need as well as being respectful of their time by quickly getting to the point. This is the same thing you want, but never get, from a telemarketer. No wonder people are cutting the cord in such large numbers.

Below are the three examples shown all together so you can see how succinctly they communicate the essence of the communication. Note that times and other information are abbreviated to the minimum number of characters to balance understanding and brevity:

- BLUF: World will end at 10p without your action. Tell me if you can meet before 6p to review options otherwise I will seek deep shelter. The enemy has threatened to launch missiles unless we accede to his demands.
- BLUF: I am applying to graduate school and am seeking your recommendation. Please let me know if you can submit the recommendation by 10 May. I have attached the necessary form for the university with my personal information.
- BLUF: Project funds will be exhausted at the end of this week at current spending level. Please call me today about sending $30M by Fri 4p. Unless you send more money, I have to stop work on this project.

It is hard to be much briefer and clearer than these examples.

As I advise throughout this book, you have to use judgment when applying the BLUF keyword to your email messages. The value of making "BLUF" the first characters of your message is it helps focus the reader's attention. It is a bright, flashing light that informs people that what follows is the most important part of the email. However, I don't always use the BLUF keyword in my messages. Sometimes I am just responding to a few questions that only require brief answers. For an email like that, a 3-sentence BLUF is probably overkill. One sentence, "Here are the answers to your questions" is probably all you need. You don't need the BLUF keyword in this instance. Some of my emails are so brief that the BLUF is all I send. In that case, I usually skip the BLUF keyword. Another reason to skip use of the BLUF keyword is sending an email to someone with whom you do not expect to communicate frequently or a non-native English speaker. In these latter two cases, introducing the BLUF keyword may confuse the recipient and it is too much work to explain the concept of a BLUF in cases like these.

Try to construct the BLUF, at least a first draft, when you first compose the body of an email. Remember, the BLUF answers the questions: What is the issue or problem? Why is the email message important? What help or action is needed? Remember steps 1 and 2 of the PAASTUB system, Purpose and Action. If you are clear about these two things, constructing the BLUF is much easier.

Don't worry about making the BLUF perfect the first time. Mine almost never are. To create an excellent, effective BLUF, you need to revisit it after you have written the email to make sure it matches what you actually wrote. Editing and improving the BLUF and your email is recursive. The BLUF helps you organize the body of your email and the body of your email makes your thoughts about the BLUF clearer.

If your email is only three to four lines, has no attachments, or needs no text after the BLUF, you could skip the BLUF keyword. Begin the message with what you want to communicate. Readers won't miss the keyword.

In the next section, you can practice the skills needed to construct BLUFs for your own emails. It takes practice to create good BLUFs because it is hard to think about the reader after you have spent a lot of time writing an email. One aspect of the skill needed to write a good BLUF is being able to focus on the most important features of an email. The practice section give you an opportunity to do that.

Practice

For the practice situations described briefly below, construct the BLUF that should accompany the email. You can check your BLUF with the one I created, but don't peak at it until you have tried to write your own. Remember that there can be many ways to convey the same information. If your BLUF is just three plus or minus one sentences and contains the same information as mine, you are on the right track.

Your BLUF should address the three key questions:
- What is this about?
- What is the action?
- Why is this important?

<u>Situations</u>

1. You are inviting several people to be guests on an episode of your podcast, "Becoming an Email Ninja." You will need to schedule the recording around their schedule, but it needs to happen between 15 and 30 September to align with your show release schedule. You will communicate in email what the hardware and software requirements are for doing the podcast recording.

BLUF: Invitation to be a guest on my podcast, "Becoming an Email Ninja" 15-30 Sept. If interested, pls email your availability for several dates and preferred times over that period. If you can do this, I will send hw+sw requirements separately.

2. You were taught a one-day workshop at a site in Europe on becoming an Email Ninja. The person that sponsored the workshop, Mr. Smith, is well-known to the recipient of the email you intend to send. The workshop went so well, you want to ask a consultant colleague if he might be interested in finding additional interested parties for the workshop. You believe this could be a good business opportunity for both of you.

BLUF: I just led an Email Ninja workshop in Europe with Mr. Smith. Would you be interested in collaborating or sponsoring me for similar work for any of your clients? This could be a good opportunity for both of us.

3. You are a member of an academic society related to your research work. When you renewed last year, you were a student and received a discounted membership rate. You were awarded your degree this year and no longer qualify for the student membership rate. You cannot determine from the website how to change your membership status from student member to regular member.

BLUF: Last year I was a student member. How do I renew as a regular member? I was awarded my doctoral degree this year. I am probably not entitled to the reduced fee.

4. You belong to many academic societies related to your research interests. The president of one of the Special Interest Groups (SIGs) of one society is seeking board members for the group. She is also seeking people to review submittals for an upcoming conference. She sent a broadcast email to the entire SIG requesting help. Since you completed your doctoral degree this year, you want to demonstrate interest in both requests. At the same time, you want to introduce yourself because she does not know you personally. This will give her an idea of what kinds of research you are most qualified or interested in reviewing.

BLUF: I am interested in serving on the SP SIG board and reviewing papers for the 2017 conference. I was awarded my doctoral degree in Sociology from the George Washington University this year. I have provided a link to my bio below.

5. You have recently been hired to assist your former employer with improving the email skills of their employees. You will conduct the

workshop 1 September. You want to inform two colleagues that know you well that you will be coming back to run a one-day workshop. You would like to get specific ideas from them about the email weaknesses of their teams because this will enable you to tailor the workshop to their needs.

BLUF: I have been hired by the company to teach a one-day workshop focused on improving email skills. Pls send me any specific concerns with your team's email skills so I can address them in the workshop. The workshop is scheduled 1 Sept.

6. You need help from two of your colleagues. You want them to recommend your for work. Instead of just asking them to recommend you, you have chosen to write a draft email they can send. In this example, write the BLUF as if the email were being sent by them, not you. You want people to know that you are a) a retired military officer and nuclear engineer, b) have a doctorate in Sociology from the George Washington University, and c) interested in doing applied qualitative research with organizations engaged in high reliability work.

BLUF: Dr. John Smith is a retired military officer and nuclear engineer. He earned a doctorate in Sociology from the George Washington University. He is interested in doing applied qualitative research with organizations engaged in high reliability work.

7. You have not heard back from one of the guests you invited to be on your podcast in example 1. His name is Bob. You are sending a followup email reminding him that he has not responded, but you have heard back from other guests so the recording dates need to be 21 or 28 March. It is now one week from the 21st and you need to know if he can participate.

BLUF: Bob, did you see my previous request? It might have slipped off your radar. Pls reply if you can support either 21 or 28 Mar, the dates that work best for the other guests? 21 Mar is just a week away and I need to the final guest list right away.

Key points from Chapter 9

- The principle behind providing a BLUF is to focus reader attention with a super concise summary at the beginning of the message.

- People get enormous amounts of electronic mail so most don't have time to read emails that don't get quickly to the point (aka "the bottom line").
- The Bottom Line Up Front (BLUF) is the elevator speech version of your email. If you only had time to explain your email to the receiver during short elevator ride, the BLUF is what you would say.
- A good rule of thumb for the length of the BLUF is three sentences.
- Your BLUF should answer three key questions, in this order, as briefly as possible:

  - What is this about?
  - What is the action?
  - Why is this important?

This is the end of Part 1, Seven Steps for Brilliant Email. The Seven Steps are habits you need to develop to improve the effectiveness of your email communications. The Seven Steps are focused on one end in mind: the reader. The Seven Steps in Part 1 represent the "program" for becoming an Email Ninja.

In Part 2 of the book, you will learn how to run the program the ways it can be tailored to improve particular types of email messages. Part 2 describes and provides example strategies and tactics of email composition and management. Chapter 10 details strategies that apply broadly across all emails. Chapter 11 provides tactics designed to make you more productive when sending the four most common types of email.

Part 2 - Email Strategies and Tactics

BLUF: Writing brilliant emails is one component of the system presented in this book. Being great at individual email composition is enhanced by using strategies tailored for the four categories of most email (Chapter 10) and high leverage tactics that you can apply within individual emails (Chapter 11). This part of the book describes the strategies and tactics of email management.

Chapter 10: Email Strategies

BLUF: Email is best managed through strategies, broad approaches that apply across all emails that promote greater effectiveness, and tactics that help you get the best results from specific types of emails. This chapter addresses email strategies and Chapter 11 covers email tactics.

Introduction

In the first part of this book, I described my system for composing brilliant emails. I broke down the system into seven steps to follow for each email you send that uses the acronym PAASTUB, which stands for Purpose is Clear, Action-What and When?, Addressees, Subject as Art, Take Out the Trash, Ugly Remarks Edited, and BLUF-ing. These are the key elements of every email message. I made the case that most bad behavior you see in email result from two things. First, people don't get taught how to communicate well using email. There is a big difference between communicating and communicating well. The training people do receive almost always focuses solely on how to use a particular email program. Second, the process flow of most email programs from "compose message" to "send" does not map well to the things you have to think about to communicate clearly. The seven steps of the PAASTUB process are the key to thinking differently about communicating effectively in email to accomplish your goals.

The second part of this book takes the seven steps of PAASTUB and adds strategies for applying them to all email (Chapter 10 Email Strategies) and then tactics for specific types of email (Chapter 11 Tactics for High-Leverage Email). This chapter begins with some ideas on email inbox management. It continues with strategies that will improve your effectiveness across all the email you send regularly.

Inbox Management

I use a simple and fast approach to manage the emails in my inbox. This section explains why my approach might be better for you too. The process I use to manage the mess that gets dropped into my inbox daily is what some people call "inbox triage." In this section, I provide a clear explanation of my strategies so you can adapt them to meet your needs.

My two themes for inbox management are **simplicity** and **speed**. They lead to what I call the 3-S Rule: Simplicity Supports Speed. I don't want to devote too much of my brain space (this is called "cognitive capacity") to a complex email and task management process. Complex processes that use folders and lots of rules are too much work for me to set up and have to be constantly tweaked. They are a distracting layer between me and making quick decisions about what to do with email. I want the simplest software interface possible in most of the programs I use. Similarly, I don't want anything getting in the way of scanning each email and the lightning-fast decisions I need to make about what to do with it.

There are several reasons why I think simpler is better for inbox management. First, a simple process is easier to remember so you are more likely to be consistent using it. The apps or rules that "pre-process" email into categories and folders are not simple for me. When I only have few minutes to do inbox triage, I only have time to look in my inbox, not a host of special folders. I can never remember where to look for messages in those special folders to find what's important. I can remember to check the inbox, trash, and spam or junk. That's it.

Second, I have found it more effective to publish email etiquette guides and provide clear expectations for the people that send me email frequently. I don't do this harshly or in the spirit of "I am the boss so do what I say," neither of which is very effective. After seeing how the guidelines work in practice, most of the people I teach love them. The small number that don't adopt the guidelines quickly need special attention, which is beyond the scope of this book. I think of setting clear expectations through email etiquette guidelines as an investment in organizational productivity. They make everyone more effective.

Third, I find third-party and complex rule-based approaches to email management cumbersome and distracting. They take too much effort to set up and require additional layers of mental processing that are not simple for me. When I have tried using rule-based email filing in the past, I always ended up sending important messages to the Trash folder. I don't know why and I never had enough time to find out.

Speed comes from using a really fast inbox scanning algorithm. The steps in my algorithm are:

- First: determine if it is one of the four types of email (event announcement or invitation, event planning, providing something, or asking for something) or something else. Recognizing the type of email helps me act on it faster.
- Second: decide whether it matters or you care (delete if you don't care, send to spam if you don't want to see more from the sender).
- Third: decide what the action is. It might just be one quick thing like a reply or it might be a group of things.
- Fourth: if email matters to you, clarify your commitment to the action needed. This is basically deciding how important the action is and how much effort you are going to put forth to accomplish it.
- Fifth: decide whether to do it now (good), delegate it to someone else (better), or do it later. If you choose to do it later, you need a simple system to manage the action to ensure you follow up like you committed. Try not to leave emails requesting action in your inbox more than a few days because it clutters your scanning process, which is not simple. I will have more to say about the system I use for managing email action in the Taking Action section of the next chapter.

The decisions I make for my inbox management process depend on several factors: how much time I have, my perceptions of the importance of the communication, and my mental energy. I have more energy and can take more aggressive action on my inbox in the morning. Mid-day, I have a lot going on so I only have time for quick replies. Later in the evening, I am not nearly as effective at deciding what to do about email so I generally only respond to important communications. What I judge to be important depends on several factors usually connected to how well I know the sender, proximity to deadlines, and providing help as soon as I can when someone asks.

There are times when the best inbox management strategy is "give up." I'm serious. If you are over a hundred messages behind and are going on vacation in two days, one of the worst things you can do is try to read them all because there might be a few "important" emails there. No matter where you are in the organizational hierarchy, devoting many hours to reading email, most of which will be low priority, just to "catch up" is not the best use of your time. You should be spending your last hours before vacation closing out projects and taking actions due before you leave the office. A good strategy in this case involves four steps.

First, search for every email from your boss and prioritize the action. This needs no further elaboration. Second, search for every email that has the "action" keyword. This is a reward to the people that are using good subjects. Decide if you can take the action before you leave for vacation. If not, inform each sender with the same brief message like "I will not be able to take this action before my leave starts on [date1]. Can you get help from somewhere else or wait until after I return?" Third, send one email to everyone except your boss with text similar to "I will be out of the office for X days starting [date1]. I can't finish reading all the messages in my inbox received after [date2]. I will come to you in the next two days so you can brief me on your most important projects, deadlines, and problems. Please have a list ready when I come so I can visit everyone in the time I have available." Fourth, delete all remaining unread email. Don't announce this in the email in step three since it may come across as too abrupt. You can tell people when you visit them that you didn't have time to read their email.

After you develop a strategy for email inbox and action management that works for you, focus on high-level approaches that are applicable for all emails. That's what the next section is about.

Strategies for All Emails

For each strategy that follows, I name the strategy, explain it, and describe how I use it to improve my effectiveness across all kinds of email. I consider the most important email strategies to be:

- Ignore all surveys,

- Which of the four types of email are you sending?
- Is email the most appropriate way to communicate?
- Stop after two emails when opinions are diverging (Two Email Rule),
- Don't send confusing emails,
- Be responsive,
- Use standard replies,
- Provide draft emails for superiors to send,
- Don't use read receipts,
- Reduce email volume when possible, and
- Teach others how to send better email.

Ignore all surveys. This is not strictly an email strategy, but it is related to all the others. Ignoring email survey requests gives you more time to focus on the important messages in your inbox. The concept is simple: don't take surveys, provide feedback on your customer experience, or explain why you want to unsubscribe from an email list. You have better things to do. I used to take almost all the surveys I was sent until I got frustrated with the dumb questions and looked for someone I could contact about them. I noticed that surveys are almost never sent by a human. The address is usually something like: "wedon'tcarewhatyouthinkofthissurvey@wasteofyourtime.com". That was when the scales fell from my eyes and I realized, "They don't really care what I think!" That was truly liberating.

I don't reply to any survey request that does not provide an estimate of how much time it is going to take (ten minutes is my limit) and a tangible reward like a chance to win something that I value, which eliminates 99% of those pesky requests. It also gives me a perverse pleasure to delete the requests without reading them. This is not easy for me because I think of myself as a nice person and the survey requests can be sooo polite. "Gee, they want to know what I think. The email says my input is valuable." If my input is valuable, why do they want it for free? Valuable is free? That does not compute.

Survey requests are like spam, telemarketing and robocalls because they are leeches on your most precious assets: time and focus. My time is too valuable to give it away to strangers that want me to answer screenfuls of questions about waiting room cleanliness. It doesn't matter how nicely their email is worded. Be decisive and move on to more important things.

Which of the four types of email are you sending? Most email messages fall into four types. Thinking about your email messages as one of these four common types is an aid for being systematic about how you handle them. It helps you focus on (1) what to convey, (2) what is most useful to others, and (3) the basic layout of the message text. You could easily think of more types than I do, but remember my preference for simple rules that are speedy to apply. As a review, I consider the four common types of email messages to be:

- Meeting or event invitations or announcements (time and date known)
- Meeting or event set up (finding a time and date depending on others' availability, providing information to support the meeting)
- Giving something
  - Information in the body of an email
  - Information in attachments, like feedback
  - Comments on someone else's email
- Asking for something
  - Request for help
  - Feedback on something
  - Asking a question
  - Action (by a deadline)

Mentally organizing emails into event announcements, event set up, giving something, and asking for something helps you use standard approaches for composing them. I will have more to say in Chapter 11 about the standard approaches and tactics for the four types. This will make you more effective with each.

Is email the most appropriate way to communicate? Another way to state this strategy is: use the best communications method to accomplish your goal. This is a "sender rule" that applies primarily to what you send, but can also be a teaching opportunity when you receive emails from others. Email is not always the most appropriate means to build mutual understanding, especially for sensitive matters that require high levels of trust. If an issue is sensitive (e.g., capable of being misunderstood by others, difficult to talk about openly, or might hurt the recipient's feelings), you probably shouldn't be sending an email. Remember from Step 5 Take Out the Trash that all criticism in email comes across more harshly than face-to-face unless you yell at someone (don't do that). An email message is just text. It has no tone of voice, no facial expressions, and is much more abrupt than most voice communication.

Email is best suited for brief, informal communications about non-controversial issues. This strategy goes deeper than the clarity of purpose you need to have when you compose an email that I covered in Chapter 3. When I believe an issue is complex or subtle, I try to call the person first to explain what I am thinking before composing an email. This saves me lots of time and allows me to convey in 5-10 minutes of talking what would take two or three screenfuls of text when done with tact. I usually only send emails or texts about complex issues if I cannot reach someone on the phone after trying several times. Even then, the email is only three to four lines long to identify the basic issue and ask when they will be available for a call. Some people seem to *think* they can do everything with texts or email. I have serious doubts about this.

Another reason to call instead of email is when planning some activity with other people that involves personal preferences, options, and identifying constraints. An example of this is planning a six-day vacation in Ireland for two couples living in different time zones, something I did recently. Even if you have the planning lead (or think you do), it is not going to be productive to do a lot of detailed planning until you review important preferences and constraints with the other couple. The best approach is to provide an itinerary or basic plan (like an agenda) and then get on the phone to discuss options and preferences. I don't try to plan anything complicated with emails. I have tried it before. It doesn't work and gets frustrating fast.

You may not realize at first how complex an issue is until you fill up an entire screen with email text. This is a really good signal that the issue is more complicated that you recognized when you began composing your email. This happens to me periodically. When it does, I take my fingers off the keyboard (stop digging the hole deeper). I then spend a few moments thinking about the key aspects of the issue and save the draft. I either send a quick note to the person to arrange a call or pick up the phone and try to call them. After speaking with them, it can be useful to send a now much shorter email with background material and specific action for follow up. This is why I save the draft before making the call.

When people that work for you send you an email about a complex topic that would require a really long reply, briefly respond with "Please call me because this is too complicated for email." Make sure you replace "Re:" in the subject with "Pls call" This will give you the opportunity to do some teaching.

Stop after two emails when opinions are diverging. I call this the **Two Email Rule** and it is a corollary of the prior strategy, "Is email the most appropriate way to communicate?" Don't argue in email. Using email to argue with someone is just as pointless as arguing face-to-face and has the added defect that it takes much longer. If you have sent two emails to someone on a particular issue and they still disagree strongly with you, don't seem to understand you, or seem to interpret your ideas much differently than you intended, take your fingers off the keyboard. It is practically guaranteed that a third email will be a waste of time. Just call or visit the person and try to work out your different views of the issue. Email is a very poor way to debate or reach mutual understanding about complex issues. These require a lot of dialog and active listening to find common ground and avoid misunderstanding. These same guidelines apply if you find yourself arguing with complete strangers in social media or forums, except for the call or visit part. In those cases, don't continue to debate with them. Just close your browser tab or window and get on with your life.

Don't send confusing emails. A "study problem" is what I call a confusing email message without clear action or purpose. A study problem requires too much work from the recipient (often me) to figure out what you are trying to communicate. *Do not send study problems*. An example of a study problem I get periodically is an email with the text "I thought you would find this interesting" and a link or a long string of emails. Busy people don't have time or the ability to read your mind to understand why you sent a study problem. If I cannot understand what the point of an email is in a minute of scanning, I stop reading. Then I reply with "I don't understand what you are trying to tell me. Could you please explain my action?" That is both clear and polite and likely motivates the sender to provide the information they should have included earlier. There is no need for a harangue or rebuke, but I usually do provide suggestions for improved email practices the next time I see the person.

When you send email, make it easy for recipients to quickly understand the issue and action, if any. If you forward an email thread, begin with the text "I sent this because ..." and finish with "This is why it is important:". Many of the practices addressed in this book like BLUF-ing, explaining forwards, and summarizing attachments help you avoid sending study problems.

Be Responsive. I try to respond as quickly as I can to any email that requests action. Fair or not, many senders expect quick replies no matter how complex the action. When the action is easy, this is no problem. When I think it might take more than a day to complete the action, I explain this in a quick, brief reply that includes an estimate for when I think I can complete the action. The quick reply lets them know that I have read the email and have a plan to do what they asked. I can also use the quick reply to tell them I cannot do it. This is important because the sender may be waiting for your reply to take other action. People notice and really appreciate this kind of responsiveness. Since a "working on it and this is my estimated completion date" reply commits you to the action, you have to be diligent about entering the action into your system for managing commitments. This is why you need an action management strategy for email.

Use standard replies. I find it useful to use templates and standard replies for issues that recur frequently. I use templates for repetitive emails such as recurring status reports. Use standard replies for topics like reminders to use better email subjects (I send those a lot), explaining what a BLUF is, and providing your personal biography (short and long versions). I have a standard, lengthy reply for social contact requests to let people know my current status and projects. Many email tools support keeping standard email in a "drafts" folder. You can copy the text from a draft email and then customize it as needed. You can use mobile or desktop note applications in a similar way with different notes saved like drafts. You can use keyboard shortcut programs that allow you to compose entire email messages with just a few keystrokes. What I like about keyboard shortcut programs is they work inside of web applications as well as email messages, but they aren't authorized in all organizations.

Provide drafts for superiors to send. There are many times when you need your boss or someone senior to you to send an email for you. Some examples are assigning action to someone senior to you (but a peer of your boss), introductory emails from your boss to someone you want to meet, and emails recommending you for some new position. After you ask your boss **in person** to do this, you should always provide a draft of the email for them. You know the issue better and you know exactly what kind of help you want. A common error people make when writing drafts for others to send is to write the email in the form of a recommendation to their boss, "I recommend you send an email to person A …" This isn't helpful because it requires extra editing by your boss to make it look like he wrote it, not you. Instead, compose the email as if you were your boss, in the first person ("I need you to do X.").

Your boss or the person senior to you may only use a fraction of your draft. Don't worry about that. Briefly summarize the issue and the action you need. Your boss will decide how much of your text to keep and express the ideas his or her own way, but your intimate knowledge of what is needed from whom and why will accelerate the process. Your boss will be able to send the email much faster with your input. The more often you do this, the better your drafts will become, particularly if your boss shares the final product with you.

Don't use read receipts. Do not request delivery and read receipts. *I think this is a very low-trust practice.* This will almost always annoy your recipient before he or she has even read your message. Besides, it often doesn't work since the recipient could have blocked that function, or his/her software might not support it, so what is the use? Some have very strong feeling about this practice and label it "evil." Do you really want to send the message "I don't trust you" with every email? Not me. If you want to know whether an email was received it is better to ask the recipient to let you or follow up with a phone call. If you think someone is ignoring your emails, you should discuss it with your supervisor, not use read receipts.

Reduce email volume when possible. I have four suggestions for reducing unnecessary emails. There are likely many more, but these will get you started. The first way to reduce email volume is don't send low priority email such as thank you's unless someone has gone way beyond what was expected. Brief "thanks" emails just add clutter and another email for the recipient to process. You can explain to people in person why you don't send thank you emails. The second way to reduce email volume is don't reply to someone that an action is complete if it is obvious that you have taken the action. For example, if someone asks you to set up a meeting, your meeting request is sufficient. Don't reply to their email, just take the action. A third way to reduce email volume is delete any extra text in replies. For example, if you get an action email, but can't take the action immediately, inform the sender that you received it. You can do this easily with a reply that inserts "got it-" at the beginning of the original subject (replacing "re:") and delete all the text in the original email. In many email clients, the message preview will be the subject and "EOF" (end of file). The recipient can just glance at the message and delete it without opening it, very easy. A fourth way to reduce email volume is changing meeting details like the date, location, or agenda in your calendar, not with an email. Anyone identified as a meeting attendee in your calendar will get an updated invitation. Just note at the top of the meeting notes box what the change was.

Teach others how to send better email. This strategy is a version of "teach a man to fish." Teaching people who email you frequently how to send better email helps you *and* them. It helps you because they will send better, clearer emails that are easier for you to process. It helps them use email more effectively and get faster responses from you. What I often do is "request permission," gently, either in email or face-to-face, to provide people email improvement recommendations. The text is "I have a list of email improvement recommendations that I share with others. Would you like me to send it to you?" If they give me permission, I use an email template that has the recommendations. Many people want to improve their communications practices and will welcome feedback if you seek their permission first.

How you go about teaching people depends a lot on the relationship you have with them. For people younger than me or who work for me, I request that they follow the principles in this book and send a short attachment or a series of emails on topics like BLUFs, putting actions all together, and better subjects. I do this a little at time so as not to overwhelm them. I also appeal to their self-interest by telling them "here is how to get the fastest responses from me." For peers, I don't tell them what to do, but demonstrate by power of example with great subjects, BLUFs, and other tactics in every email I send. It may take a while for them to change, but they often do. For superiors or people that have made it clear that they think they are my superiors, I don't offer any suggestions to improve their email unless they ask me. Trying to teach someone senior to you to "improve" is not a recipe for success. Teaching others to improve their email can be high leverage, but be very gentle and use sensitivity, style, and wit whenever possible. From personal experience, I have learned that brute force is not an effective way to get someone to change.

The next section has examples of the

Teach Others Examples

I can't provide concise examples of most of the strategies in this chapter because they are ways to *think* about email and not ways to actually compose messages. Just practice a few strategies at a time and you will pick them up quickly.

Below are examples of email subjects and body text that I use to teach others to improve their email. These are suitable for putting in your drafts folder after you customize them for your communications style. The notes in brackets, [ ], are notes to readers of this book and are not meant to be sent to others.

Subject Improvement Suggestions

Subj: Rob composing subjects badly [using humor as a gentle "poke" is both attention getting and less critical]

Subj: Ugly subject-(their prior subject)

Subj: Yikes-crazy subject-2:20 good: Time for check in chat today?

[corrected version of their original, really bad subject, which was "chat?"]

Message Text to Accompany Subject Improvement Suggestions

Disclaimer: I have learned that some people do not take suggestions for email improvement well. If you are one of those types, stop reading now. If you are not one of those types, but get offended easily or have no intention of changing, those are also good reasons to stop reading and ignore the text that follows. [Using some humor before introducing better practices works well]

BLUF: Please consider using more specific email subjects. I ruthlessly screen emails by subject and open those with the clearest action first. Below are tips for thinking differently about email that will significantly improve my ability to help you in the future.

Most people screen emails by subject and I am no exception. The quicker I understand the action you need from me, the quicker I can provide it or tell you when I can provide it.

You may have noticed that I almost always change the subject when I believe the original one no longer applies (or to put it more gently, "when the original subject is less applicable"). What I would have suggested for your email is something along the lines of:

Subj: (better subject here) [This is where you can provide a concrete example]

BLUF: This is the Bottom Line Up Front of your message. The BLUF is the essence of your email content, including action and due date, in three or fewer sentences. If you can describe what you want and when or what your email is about in a single, simple sentence, that is even better.

For example, for your email, my BLUF would have been: (insert BLUF here) [another concrete example]

Always ask yourself, "will my recipient(s) know what I want or am providing *from the subject alone*?" It is common to use a placeholder subject or compose an email and leave actions at the bottom as you slowly, gently build to your point (to keep the email from coming across as harsh). What is uncommon is to review the email before sending to make sure that you collect all the actions, place them after the BLUF, and ensure the first sentence of the BLUF summarizes the action and due date in a single sentence *before* hitting "send." [If applicable, you can insert: You are learning, I have noticed.]

The general guidelines I have developed for an excellent subject: no more than 40 characters; replace the "re" in the front of replies with things like "can do" or "here it is" in response to requests; put any text you add to the original subject at the beginning, in place of "re" so it won't get truncated; change the subject as soon as it no longer describes the message content, and use keywords at the beginning of the subject like "alert," "action," and "need help" when applicable to get extra attention, if desired.

Another useful tip is to put all the actions you want in one place, near to top, right below the Bottom Line Up Front (BLUF). That is extremely helpful for busy recipients like me.

Positive Reinforcement

When someone is making subject or email composition progress, you should point this out in your replies. Positive reinforcement for change goes a long way for changing behavior. How else do bears learn to ride bicycles?

Subj: getting the handle on great subjects, well done (their prior subject)
Subj: Really nice subject-(their prior subject)
Subj: Great Subject-(their prior subject)
BLUF: Well done subject. It jumped to near the top of my "do right now" list because of it.

Key points from Chapter 10

- My **3-S** rule is the foundation for all the email strategies in this chapter: Simplicity Supports Speed. The email strategies suggested in this chapter apply for the all the emails you send.
- Emails generally fall into four types: event invitations and announcements, event planning, taking action, and requesting action. You can compose better email messages more systematically if you keep the needs of each type at the forefront as you draft them. General strategies for all four types of email: be responsive, use standard replies, no flaming, provide drafts, don't bother with receipts. Specific tactics for being more effective within each of the four types are discussed in the next chapter.
- Email is not always the most appropriate way to communicate. Issues and actions related to complex or sensitive topics that people have passionate and deeply-held beliefs about should be discussed over the phone or face-to-face before sending an email. If your first email on a topic exceeds one screen in length, you should probably pick up the phone before proceeding.
- The "two-email rule" is another way to think about the folly of arguing in email. If you detect wide differences between you and your recipient after two emails, pick up the phone.
- Don't send email study problems to recipients, which ask the recipient to figure out what you are trying to convey or the

action you are requesting. The purpose of BLUFs (Step 7 of the PAASTUB process, addressed in chapter 9) and explaining attachments and forwards (see chapter 11) is to make it easy for recipients to quickly understand the issue and necessary action.

- Respond as quickly as you can to requests for action. Email senders have a tendency to assume that the email they just sent is the most important and interesting thing in your inbox. If you cannot take action right away, send a note about this with either an estimate of when you can take the action and stating that you cannot take the action.

- Use standard messages and template for issues that come up again and again: personal introductions, brief biographies, repetitive requests you make, social media connection replies, teaching other people to send better email, etc. Using templates for repetitive issues saves lots of time.

- Provide drafts of any email you want someone else to send on your behalf. You know the topic better than anyone and know exactly what you need so save the other person from the "blank screen-blank mind" black hole. You are likely to get faster action by providing a draft to review.

- Don't bother with send or read receipts. They are low trust and many email clients allow recipients to bypass them. If you think someone is routinely ignoring your emails, this is something you should be discussing with your supervisor.

- Reduce the volume of email you send by not sending "thank you" emails. Only thank someone for going above and beyond what you expected.

- Take advantage of opportunities to teach others to send more effective email. If you expect to get a lot of email from someone, consider really bad subjects or actions at the bottom of the the email as teachable moments. Gently explain, don't criticize, how they can be more effective with email by using standard messages about BLUFs, actions, and subjects. Consider getting "permission" from them first before trying to help them improve.

Chapter 11: Tactics for High-Leverage Email

BLUF: Email tactics are high-leverage practices that improve your productivity and effectiveness within messages. The tactics integrate all of the steps of the PAASTUB process and include my additional insights about communication to improve the effectiveness of your email even further. There are also tactics you can apply within each of the four types of email that will make them even better.

Introduction

This chapter explains the email tactics that I find most useful, but seldom see practiced by others. The tactics are focused on designing your messages to improve your ability to accomplish your goals. Email Ninjas use these tactics for every email they send:

- Update subjects frequently,
- Write about others cautiously,
- Criticize gently,
- Make humor explicit,
- Be cautious with Bc (Blind Copy),
- Explain forwarded messages,
- Summarize every attachment,
- Single topic per message,
- Use whitespace to improve readability,
- Drop "dear all,"
- Keep signatures short,
- Get permission for large attachments,
- Don't recall messages,
- Don't send SPAM (or waste people's time),
- Learn to search well, and
- Do a final review before sending.

After explaining each tactic, I follow up with several more focused on particularly good things to do when sending each of the four main types of emails identified in the last chapter:

1) meeting invitations and announcements,
2) meeting set up,
3) giving something,
4) asking for something.

Taken together, the integration of the PAASTUB process with the tactical insights from this chapter will sharpen your focus on message recipients, making you more productive and effective.

Tactics for High-Leverage Email

Update subjects frequently. As noted in chapter 6, always use clear, brief, focused subjects in your email. If someone sends you an email with a terrible subject ("meeting"), you don't have to pass on the problem by using it in a reply or forward. So don't do it. Make the choice to be creative and interesting, not thoughtless and lazy. You don't want to be thoughtless and lazy.

There are two important reasons to change the subject when you reply. The first is to provide a clear example for the sender and others on distribution. The utility of more specific and focused subjects might not be obvious right away, but people do notice the difference because your messages will stand apart from everything else in their inbox. In my experience, many people notice AND start improving their subjects just by your example. If the sender is a peer or senior to you, that's the best you can hope for. The second reason is that the email string may go back and forth many times with more than one change in topic. If you change a subject that was originally "Meeting" to "Mtg-27 Sep 1p, Conf Rm 2 re dog kennels" and later to "Need help, dog kennel mtg agenda-27 Sep," that is a huge improvement for everyone's inbox.

Some people have the opinion that it is a bad practice to change email subjects. Their logic is that this makes it harder to search for emails by subject and follow a series of messages. I still think it is a good practice to change email subjects when you reply or forward. Many people that haven't read this book NEVER change email subjects on reply. If you reply quickly to a group with your modified subject, your subject becomes the de facto standard that everyone uses from then on. That doesn't impact the bad practices of others (at least not right away), but it certainly improves your inbox and actually improves your searches. Instead of searching for "meeting," you can search for "27 Sep."

It is especially important no to reuse old email subjects when the topic has changed. It drives me bonkers when people do this, especially when the original subject started with "URGENT" and is no longer urgent. As discussed in Chapter 6, the subject should always reflect the content of the email you are sending *right now*. For example, if someone asks me to do something, such as "Need help-ltr of rec by 1 Dec," my response will typically use a subject like "will do-Need help-ltr of rec by 1 Dec" instead of "re: Need help-ltr of rec by 1 Dec." **Reminder**: when you add text to an email subject, always add it at the *beginning* to keep it from getting truncated.

Here are two examples taken from my inbox that illustrates both Step 4 Subject as Art and the value of updating subjects as the "conversation" changes:

Example 1

Original subject of email I received: "cell phone"

The email was in response to my request for a person's cell phone number. In the body of the email, the sender also asked for the dates I would be in his country. Thus a better subject from this sender would have been: "cell ph+when coming?"

My reply subject was: "21-27 Mar Ralph in Spain"

His reply subject was "RE: 21-27 Mar Ralph in Spain"

In the reply, the sender asked which day we could meet. A better subject for him to use would have been: "meet 25 or 26? 21-27 Mar Ralph in Spain". Notice "RE" should have been removed and the new information inserted at the beginning of the subject. There was not need to add "Mar" since it was obvious.

My reply subject was: "meet 3-25, Sat? 21-27 Mar Ralph in Spain"

His reply subject was": RE: meet 25 Mar, Sat? 21-27 Mar Ralph in Spain"

In this reply, the sender asked what time we should meet. A better subject would have been: "lunch or dinner, time? meet 25 Mar." Notice I dropped off "21-27 Mar Ralph in Spain" since it was unnecessary at this point. My standard practice is to remove anything in the subject that does not need to be there.

My reply subject was was: "Dinner? meet 25 Mar, Sat"

His reply was subject: "RE: Dinner? meet 25 Mar, Sat"

In the reply, the recipient said he would meet me at the train station at 15:00.

My reply subject was: "Great: meet train station, 1500 25 Mar, Sat"

The pattern is clear. One of us created a very specific subject for each email. The other didn't. I could have sent my partner an email explaining why my approach to email subjects was better than his, but this was a highly educated colleague that I didn't know well enough to do this. I did not want to risk offending him and damaging our relationships by sending him something that he might interpret as criticism. Unfortunately, email just works that way. Smart people almost always "come around" to seeing the value of updated subjects. It just takes some longer than others so be patient.

Example 2

The original subject of an email I received had the subject: "update and request".

The email contained a request to "meet" via the phone. It even included the times and days of the sender's availability, which was great. I have taught this person about email subjects in the past.

My reply subject was: "Happy to help, call Wed 1100: update and request"

I could have just used "call Wed 1100," but adding "Happy to help" made it more enthusiastic and fun for me. That is a piece of the "art" that should be embedded in your email subjects whenever possible. At the same time, I sent this person a meeting request. In the "location" field of the meeting, I entered "Bob calls Ralph at [my number]." I could have just sent the meeting request without an email reply, something I often do for people I know well.

Write about others cautiously. I covered this in Chapter 8, Step 6: Ugly Remarks Edited, but it is so important that it worth some extra emphasis here as an Email Ninja tactic. Even though writing an email feels like a private communication, it is not. Not even close because you have no control over it after you "send." The feeling you have of "this is just between us" is an illusion. When writing about others, always imagine they are going to read what you have written. Because email is so easy to forward, they likely *will* read what you wrote because someone else will forward it to them. This means that you should never speak ill of others in email no matter how much you think they really deserve it. This is the electronic, semi-permanent, you-have-no-control-of-what-the-receiver-does equivalent of talking badly about others behind their back. In my view, making disparaging remarks about others is a low trust and unprofessional practice. It reflects badly on you whether you do it in person or via a keyboard. If you really think someone deserves a stern rebuke, have the moral courage to look them in the eye when you deliver it. A great way to protect yourself from "slippage" in this area is to include any person you are mentioning in the email on the distribution as soon as you realize you are writing about them. I do this all the time. This gives the person a chance to provide feedback on what you write and helps you behave. When I do this, I can almost imagine the person looking over my shoulder as I write.

Don't pass on criticism from others. If someone else speaks evil of others and that email message arrives in your inbox, do two things when you reply. First, "soften" their language before you send your reply so others won't be offended or hurt. Another option is just eliminate the remarks entirely. Just because someone else "steps in it," you don't have to spread it around. I showed classy ways to do this in Chapter 7, Take Out the Trash. Second, forward the email with the softer language back to the person that sent it to you, if junior to you, and remind them that criticizing others in email is a bad practice. If the critical comment sender is a peer or senior to you and takes the time to read your entire message with their criticism edited, they will figure it out.

Criticize gently. Never, never, never rebuke or (harshly criticize) your email recipient. This is also called "flaming." Keeping strongly negative statements and criticism out of email messages is step 6 of the PAASTUB process, Ugly Remarks Edited. I discussed this idea at length in chapter 8, but I consider it so important that it is worth focusing on it as a distinct tactic that applies across all emails. Be vigilant for negative statements and even what you consider to be "mild" criticism whenever you about to send an email.

If you must criticize or provide suggestions for improvement, do so very gently because written criticism without tone of voice or body language feels much stronger to the recipient than you might intend. If you did intend it, go back and read Chapter 8 again. If someone sends you a tangled mess of ideas, vague actions or buries the desired action at the bottom of a long email, don't complain. Reply briefly instead about being confused, not understanding what they want, or restating the action in the first sentence to clarify. Once you get clarity, then you can point out that that burying the action makes it harder for you to help them. Transform what could be interpreted as criticism about *them* into a statement about *what you need to be more productive* and *help them*. I have found that this kind of feedback is much more readily accepted by others.

Make humor explicit. Because of the informal nature of many email communications, humorous remarks and irony can be very helpful. I use both whenever I can. Making humorous statements in email messages carries some risk, however, because what you think is obviously amusing may not be amusing to others. One way to make it clear that something you wrote was intended to be funny or ironic is to add an emoticon like a smiley face. A quick shortcut, since I often don't want to pause to look up and choose an emoticon from the thousands now available, is to simply follow the sentence with "(smile)" or "(joke)."

Be cautious with Bc. Bc stands for "blind copy," but unlike cc ("carbon copy"), no one but the sender can see the addresses of people on Bc distribution. The best and only good reason for using Bc is when you are sending an email message to more than 10 people. Sadly, many senders don't consider a full page of email addresses copied into their reply as clutter so they just leave them there. They must be oblivious to the fact that their recipients have to scroll through screenfuls of address trash to read the message after it has been forwarded several times. Distributing messages to many recipients via Bc is helpful because the email header and subsequent replies are not cluttered with all the addresses. This is what I would call a *good motive* for using Bc as long as you alert readers to it at the top of the message ("I am using Bc to reduce address clutter.").

A *bad and low-trust motive* for using Bc is trying to keep some people informed without letting anyone on distribution know. I think this a bad practice for several reasons. First, it is sneaky and probably not very ethical to be secretly informing others. Sneaky behavior carries great risk of embarrassment when (it is usually when, not if) it is discovered. Second, this is not what people expect and it may not be very clear to the person you Bc why you are doing this and what you expect from them. This is contrary to step 1 of the PAASTUB process, Purpose is Clear. If you need to keep someone informed about what you are doing, it is better to forward the email to them *after you send it* with a short note that explains your reason for forwarding it. You should be explicit about why you think they need to know. Don't use this forward as an opportunity to criticize or write disparaging things about anyone in the original email, however. Remember what you learned from step 6 of the PAASTUB process, Ugly Remarks Edited. Third, some email clients may allow the person that was Bc'd to "reply to all" which gives the whole game away. I have made this error several times.

Explain forwarded messages. This tactic is an addition to the "Send no Study Problems" strategy from Chapter 10. Your familiarity with an issue, called the Curse of Knowledge, can fool you into thinking that your reasons for forwarding the message are obvious. They aren't. This is especially true for someone swimming in their own tangled swamp of emails quickly scanning their messages. Forwarding an email without explanation is like depositing a baby on someone's porch without a note, a bad practice.

Every time I forward an email or add someone new to a reply, I use a new Bottom Line Up Front (BLUF) to explain: 1) why I forwarded the message and 2) the issues involved. This summary helps the new people and is a good review for those are already in the "conversation." I use text like, "I added Bob to this message because he is an expert in dog grooming. He can advise us on removing the smelly substance Buffy rolled in." When I add new people to an existing email thread, I nearly always update the subject in accordance with Step 4, Subject as Art. What might have been an adequate subject for existing participants is seldom sufficient for someone completely new to the conversation. This is a **huge** departure from common practice because of its focus on the reader. It makes your communications distinctly better than others.

Summarize all attachments. The corollary to explaining forwarded messages is always summarize the contents of the attachments in your emails, yours and anyone else's. "See attachments" is not the way to do this because it requires the reader to open attachments to understand key points or action. Key points and action belong in the BLUF. Clear communications require that every email message with attachments list the name of the attachment, a brief summary of the content, and why you included it. I find that the best place for this is right after the BLUF.

Single topic per message. I try to stick to a single topic and its related actions per email whenever I can. It might be more efficient for you to put a laundry list of actions and ideas in a single email, but this seldom meets the needs of the reader. The actions you give someone might fall across a spectrum from "quick and easy" to "hard and takes a lot of time." They could pertain to different projects or topics.

Organize your actions by project or topic and use separate messages for each. Using a single topic for each email is better for recipients because 1) the actions (don't forget due dates!) are clearly grouped by the topic or project in their inbox and 2) they can delete or archive each email when its actions are complete. When recipients use their inbox as a holding area for open actions (bad idea, see Ch 10, Inbox Management for better alternatives), this is very helpful.

I sometimes send two or three emails in a row to the same person for different actions and topics. Because email is practically free to send, there is no need to economize by jamming all your ideas and actions in one message. For people that don't know me well and might be surprised about getting three messages from me in succession, I explain why I do this in the first email. I use text similar to "I grouped the actions by topic and sent separate emails for each instead of one. I find this much easier for task management and I hope you do too."

Use whitespace to improve readability. Don't dump all your ideas into one long paragraph. When you need to send an email that occupies more than one screen of a mobile device, about five sentences, use paragraphs, whitespace, and headings to make it easier to read. Look at this example:

BLUF: This message is about this issue. The issue is important for this reason. I recommend these actions: (note: provide a summary, not a list, to keep the BLUF short).

Actions Recommended:
* Action 1 (date, responsible party)
* Action 2 (date, responsible party)

Attachments

The Problem

Possible Impact

Headings and blank space between paragraphs make your email much easier to scan and make the important things like actions and recommendations stand out for the reader. Some email programs "helpfully" remove all lines without text so you have to type a space on every blank line for your whitespace to survive this feature. Other types of formatting are useful, such as bullets for actions, but don't get carried away with colors, bold, italics, and emoticons. Keep it simple because special characters and icons might not transfer well between email systems. I use "*" (asterisks) as my bullets for lists. I bold words *this* way. You can _underline_ this way, but I seldom do this. *Asterisks* are good enough most of the time.

Drop "dear all." An Email Ninja manages the reader's focus. "Dear All" just wastes space. Email is informal enough that you can dispense with the "Dear" part entirely, which is just a legacy of the days of paper letters. Just get to the point. This is not abrupt and actually more respectful of the recipients' time and attention. Most email clients provide a brief preview of the messages in their inbox. Wasting characters on "Dear All" just truncates the preview of your BLUF. *That's* the first thing you want people to see in the preview. Start with the BLUF keyword and drop "Dear."

Keep signatures short. Signatures should be no more than 2-3 lines. They should consist of just your name, organization and its URL, email address, and phone number. These don't have to be on separate lines, but separation with commas is a good idea. No philosophy, quotes from your favorite cartoonist, graphics, mission statement, marketing, or links to your favorite podcast.

The rationale for short email signatures is simple: long signatures just clutter messages, making them harder to read. Any message that has been replied to several times or forwarded contains an enormous amount of message "trash" in signatures. Don't commit errors like this or pass them on (Chapter 7, Step 5: Take Out the Trash).

Don't be seduced by the ease of signature automation to include pithy quotes from Mother Teresa or Plato at the bottom of every single emails. Once, this *might* be cute or interesting. After the first email to the same person(s), they are just tedious. *Don't be tedious.* This is good guidance for getting along well with others.

Most email clients can be set up to automatically attach a default signature or file to the end of all outgoing messages. This spells trouble because "automatically" often leads to "thoughtless." If you are certain people will be impressed by your erudition from fifteen lines of text at the bottom of your email, fine, but only include it in the *first* reply and *delete it entirely* when you communicate with people that know you. They already know your favorite cartoonist.

The shortest possible email signature is none at all. You don't need to add a signature to every single email you send, especially for emails sent to close colleagues, friends, or those that are really short. There are few things more silly or tedious than sending an email message with a longer signature than the actual message text. Don't laugh, it happens all the time. I think many people either don't think about this, are in love with their Mother Theresa quote, or think it is too abrupt to send an email without a signature. Get over it. Email is not a formal letter. In most cases, it is *supposed* to be brief and informal. That's one of its great features.

Get permission for large attachments. Sharing documents, pictures, articles, presentations, etc. is great, but don't abuse the practice. Mailing a simple 100K attachment is harmless enough, but when you need to send files larger than 5 megabytes, get permission from recipients first or just send a link. Many network administrators place restrictions on the size of messages a user is allowed to receive. When someone sends an enormous attachment, it may lock the the receiver out of his mailbox. This is especially a problem when people go out of town and have to manage their inbox with a mobile device.

Don't recall messages. Don't bother trying to recall messages, ever. Chances are that your message has already been delivered and read before you can recall it so it is often a waste of time and attracts potentially undesired attention. First, there is no clearer "I am a Dumbo" flag in mail inboxes than a message titled "Ralph Soule attempted to recall ..." Recipients may eventually conclude that you *are* a dumbo, but don't make easy for them. Second, recipients may find "Ralph Soule attempted to recall" messages puzzling and intriguing because they may wonder what your error was and waste time trying to find out. You really want them to spend time reading the revised message.

Instead of recalling flawed messages, it is better just to send an email with the corrected information and a statement that you have made a mistake. When I do this, I use the subject keyword "Correction" in front of the original subject. "Boo-boo: 2nd try" or "Oops-" work too. In the second message, I use a single sentence before the BLUF to explain the general reason for the correction. This is much more professional with less potential for confusion. Don't provide too much information (TMI), however. "I left something out" or "I left some people off distribution" or "I forgot the attachment" are good enough.

Some email clients have a feature that gives you time to catch errors before they leave your account. It goes by various names, but it gives you the option of sending your email after a brief, user-specified delay. This is sometimes called "delayed send." If you do an internet search with the name of your email client followed by "delayed send," you may find instructions for managing this feature. Delayed send gives you a short interval to catch your error before transmitting the message. The mental lightning flash corresponding to "Rats, I forgot something in that email" often occurs the split second *after* you hit send. A delay of about thirty seconds is sufficient for me to catch and correct most of my biggest email crass mistakes. During the delay, your message sits in a temporary location waiting for you to reopen and edit it.

Don't send SPAM (or waste people's time). Don't forward jokes, chain letters, and second amendment appeals to anyone, ever. People get enough junk in their inbox. Be a force for good, not part of the problem.

Never email links with short, cryptic messages like, "I thought you would be interested in this" because that's exactly what the "bad people" do. Phishing emails are just generic text like "I thought you would be interested in this" followed by a link that either melts your computer, ransoms control of your control of your computer, or directs you to send money to a foreign country. My general rule is **never** open links from others, even family, unless they explain in detail why they sent it. Even then, I still usually don't follow the link (don't tell my family!). "I thought you would be interested" doesn't qualify. People do this so thoughtlessly that they seldom follow up to ask about your reaction so deletion without reading is low risk. If someone does ask for feedback, you can just tell them about the rule. If you are worried about the friction this might cause in your relationship, tell them it's **my** rule. I can handle it.

Sometimes you need to send a link in email. No problem, just follow this guideline: explain what the link is and why you sent it in enough detail that makes its utility clear. You should also add that you have personally visited the site and it did not trigger any browser security warnings.

Learn to search well. Learn how to use the search function of your email client really well. I don't mean basic search, but advanced search ("advanced find" in Microsoft Outlook). Advanced search typically allows you to search within emails and not just subjects. I could devote an entire chapter of this book to strategies for advanced search, filing email, and managing employer-imposed storage limitations, but I won't because the possible approaches are practically limitless. My system for email search is based on just three ideas.

The first idea for searching well: limit the places to search. Many highly-organized people swear by having lots of folders and tags. I have tried doing this, but it just creates complexity I don't want to manage. So many emails can be filed under more than one topic that the concept of "the right topic" is very hard to apply in practice. I prefer to direct my focus elsewhere.

Folders are useful and I use the smallest number of folders possible. This is a consequence my 3S strategy: Simplicity Supports Speed. My first two folders are the default sent and deleted folders of the email system. Nothing special here because every system has them.

Next are my three archive folders: sent, deleted, and "really deleted." My rule is that anything older than a month gets archived off line so it doesn't count against my system limit. Sent and deleted off-line folders just mimic the system folders. No thinking required for what goes there. You might need to organize the folders by year if you work somewhere for a long time.

The "really deleted" archive is not an archive in the traditional sense of keeping the contents for a long time. It is an off-line, temporary parking place for messages before I deleted them permanently. I use the "really deleted" off-line folder for two kinds of messages. First, emails I sent that had really big attachments so they don't count against storage limits. I put large messages in "really deleted" within a few days of sending them. Since I have the original attachments, there is no reason to save the messages for the long term. If I think the message text was particularly eloquent, I can reply to myself only, which puts just the message text in the sent folder for later archiving. The second type of email that goes in "really deleted" are those I received with really big attachments. You have to decide what "really big" means in your context, but I consider it anything bigger than 40k. I discard the contents of the "really deleted" folder every three months. If no one asks me about an email in three months, it isn't important enough to save.

The second idea for searching well: save all important attachments to your normal file storage area. Saving attachments separately from emails gives you fewer places to look for files, simplifying search. In other words, it decouples email search from email system storage limitations. Make sure you use really distinctive, clear filenames because this facilitates searching.

The third idea for searching well: make sure every email you send or delete has an excellent subject. The control you have over your own subjects is obvious. You likely have more control over the subjects of emails you receive than you think.

First, an undocumented feature of the Outlook desktop client is that you can change the subject of an email from someone else. This is a powerful aid to future search. Providing specific details for enabling this capability is beyond the scope of this book, but you can find guidance for doing it if you do an internet search like "outlook edit subject of received email".

Second, if your system does not allow you change the subjects of received emails directly, do it indirectly. Forward the email to yourself, without attachments, with a better subject. File this message in the deleted system folder, not sent, since you are just improving a message that someone sent to you. You aren't taking ownership of it.

In summary, teach yourself how to use the advanced search feature of your email client because searching is faster than filing. Being skilled at search requires less mental effort than creating and maintaining a complex folder or message tagging system. Follow three key ideas: keep it simple and use just the number of folders you need and no more, save email attachments where you save all documents, and give every email you save an excellent subject.

Do a final review before sending. When you think you are "done" composing your email message, do a final review. Make sure it has a clear focus on the receiver and gets right to the point. A thoughtful final review will always uncover typos, gaps in your thinking, and other barriers to effective communication. If it doesn't, your message is only two sentences or you aren't doing it carefully enough to spot missed punctuation and fragmented thoughts that can make you look barely literate to readers. Sure, email is informal, but people will judge you anyway. As you do the final review, follow a checklist like this (included as a tool in Chapter 12):

- Do you provide the action due date in **both** the subject and the BLUF? If there are different dates, use the earliest one.
- Are all the actions grouped immediately after the BLUF?
- Is the message text consistent first with the subject and second with the BLUF? They must support each other. It is very common to introduce new things in the text that you didn't include in the first draft of the BLUF so fix that when you finish composing.
- Does the BLUF cover what the email is about, what the action is, and why it is important?
- Is the action or idea clear from the subject alone? If not, make it so.
- Have you tried to use punctuation and humor in your subject while keeping its length under 30 characters?
- Is there sufficient background information after the actions to understand what needs to be done?
- Did you answer all the questions you were asked? You might have to dig into the original message again.
- Are the contents of all attachments summarized?
- Did you include as recipients all the people that have action or are mentioned in the message? Did you write about anyone or any organization not represented on distribution (that would be bad)?

Some people are going to roll their eyes at the idea of doing a final review. They may be thinking: "He recommends all this care and attention to content before *actually sending*? Sending email will take *forever!*" - or something close. A few people were bold enough to actually say this to me when I taught them my process, bless their little honest hearts. Before you throw the book (don't blame me if you break something), delete it from your e-reader, or dismiss the final review as unreasonable, consider the following:

- The final review is not only a tactic, it is an important skill for an Email Ninja. Like any skill, performance becomes faster and better with practice. Put the review steps on a card near your computer until you have them memorized.
- The final review is a skill for communicating more professionally. It is a bad practice to confuse or irritate your readers with incomplete thoughts, typos, and logic gaps (e.g.

"and then a miracle occurs"). Don't believe that nonsense about email being so informal that no one cares about your errors. As I noted earlier, *readers are going to judge you as much by how you write as what you write.*

- I usually re-read the email text, the BLUF, and the subject two or three times to make sure they support each other. I always find problems and you will too.
- For any email message longer than 3 lines, your clarity of purpose and expression will evolve as you compose it. This is a natural part of the writing process. The final review helps you get things straight as the process nears its end.
- *Don't be grumpy.* Accept the final review as an important and really useful aspect of making yourself clear and focusing on what the reader needs to take the action you need. Is taking some extra time to do this such a bad thing?

Tactics for the Four Types of Email Messages

As I noted in Chapter 10, almost all work emails are one of four types:

- meeting or event announcements,
- meeting or event set up (like agendas),
- giving something (taking action, providing information), and
- asking for something (assigning action or asking for help).

First I address emails related to meetings and general calendar events. Following the tactics for meeting emails, I provide guidance for action emails, both taking and assigning.

Meeting Requests and Announcements

For the rest of this section, I refer to all calendar related activities involving more than one person as "meetings" even though some might be luncheons, social gatherings or training announcements.

Meeting Requests and Announcements

The first decision to make about a meeting is what kind of meeting it is. Not all meetings are the same. An Email Ninja separates meeting emails into two kinds: requests and announcements. This distinction is important because different tactics are applicable to each.

Meeting Requests

These are also called invitations by some email clients. A meeting *request* is what you send when there is a specific list of people, typically fewer than ten, that must be present to accomplish the purpose of the meeting. The benefit of meeting requests is that most email clients keep a record of who has accepted the meeting and who has not. This helps you target follow up emails to just those people who have not replied.

Meeting Announcements

A meeting *announcement* is what you send when you are informing a large group or distribution list about the meeting or event, but their attendance is not mandatory. Use announcements if you do not need to know exactly who is attending the meeting (see RSVP tactics later in the chapter). You want people to know the event is happening so they have an *opportunity* to attend, but it won't be a problem if they don't. This could be training or a social activity.

The second decision you have to make about meeting emails is how to communicate about the meeting to others. This can get very complicated depending on what kind of software you and your recipients use. I want to make this book "app-nostic" as much as possible. It just is not possible to explain the best way to communicate about your meeting without going into some calendar app specifics so I have placed that information at the end of this section.

Next, I describe the details to get clear about for meeting requests and announcements to make your emails useful to others.

Arranging date and time. *The two most important things for setting up a meeting is when deciding when it will happen and who has to be there.* Finding a time and date when all necessary participants can attend is usually the hardest part of meeting management. There are many web-based tools for doing this, but most require logging into a site or learning a new tool. This may be easy for *you* to do, but convincing others to learn and use some new app or tool can be a challenge. If you can *require* all participants to use the tool, great. But why bother? It is simpler and faster to use an email to solicit availability for a meeting.

I take a "less is more" approach to arranging meetings. I send participants a brief email asking them to tell me when they are available over a certain date range. Since this is an action email, I include a due date in the subject and email body (e.g. Subject: (due 13 Nov) Pls provide dates for planning mtg). The briefer and more compelling your subject is, the greater the likelihood that recipients will respond quickly. In the email body, I *specifically request* recipients to "reply to all" because it narrows the options for the people that respond later. The key for meeting scheduling is getting quick responses so you can move on to other things like agendas and material to read before the meeting. There is a template for an event arrangement email in Part 3 of this book, Tools.

If there are large differences in status or organizational hierarchy among attendees, find out when the most senior people are available first because a) they have the busiest calendars and b) junior people just have to adapt their calendars to them. It is often faster and easier to do this by checking with the admin assistant of a senior attendee on the telephone rather than using email. In many cases, you can ask a senior person's admin assistant to work with his or her peers to find a date for the meeting when more than one senior person is involved. Always explain to the admin assistant why the meeting is important for their boss to attend and ask really nicely for their help. Both of these things are very important for getting the help you need to set up the meeting.

If you are scheduling a meeting or call with just a few people and yourself, always send your availability for the meeting in the first email. For example, you might notice that a call would be very useful after exchanging several emails on a topic. This could be because the topic is complicated or you are trying follow the Two Email rule because perspectives are diverging (see Chapter 10 if you need to review the Two Email Rule). Telling the recipient when you are available for the meeting lets them to reply just *once* with a day and time that suits both your schedules. It amazes me how few people seem to understand this. They just send emails with text like "let's talk soon/sometime." Don't do this. Follow the "let's talk" idea with some simple text like "We should talk. I am available Thursday and Friday after 2 pm. I can provide more options if neither day works." Once the recipient has chosen a date that matches your availability, follow up with a meeting request.

If you use a calendar application to enter the details of the meeting, you should use the notes section of the meeting to indicate the time of the meeting in all the time zones involved. Calendar applications are supposed to manage time zones automatically, but sometimes they don't.

For some virtual meetings, I will be in a different time zone on the day of the meeting than the one I was when I set it up. For example, I sent email invitation when I was in San Francisco, but I planned to be in London on the day the meeting. Relying on the calendar application to do the time conversion can get confusing. Putting the time of the meeting in the notes field for all the applicable time zones accomplishes two things: it is a reference point for you and lets the invitees correct your math if you made a time zone conversion error.

Meeting title. Just like email subjects, your meeting title should be as specific and short as possible. Your aim is for the meeting purpose to be clear from the title when someone glances at it on their electronic calendar. The title should be meaningful to all parties, not just you.

Whenever I schedule a call with someone, I use a title that will be meaningful for *both* our calendars. For example, I use a title like "Ralph-Bob talk Chpt 5". If I used "Talk w/Bob Chpt 5" or worse "Bob" as the title, *that's* what would show up on Bob's calendar. If Bob glances at his electronic calendar, "Bob" or "Talk w/ Bob Chpt 5" as a meeting title won't be very helpful. The title needs to be short because calendar meeting titles can get truncated shorter than email subjects, at least in some views. In the browser-based calendar app I use, "Ralph-Bob talk Chpt 5" was truncated to "Ralph-Bob talk C." For this meeting, I shortened the title to "Ralph-Bob Ch 5."

The number of characters displayed in a meeting title depends on many variables, but a good rule of thumb is to keep the title less than 15 characters, when possible. If you cannot do that, at least keep the first 15 characters very meaningful. The truncation can be even worse with laptop-based calendar applications if there is another event at the same time, like a spouse's appointment if you share calendars.

There are several other tactics for designing great meeting titles. If attendance at the meeting is mandatory, make that the first word in the meeting title. If these mandatory events happen often, start the title with "Mandatory" or "Mando." If the meeting is optional and you don't think it will be obvious to people, begin the title with "Optional" or "Opt." Avoid prepositions, conjunctions, and other unnecessary words in titles. Instead of "Ralph and Sheila Dinner," use "Dinner Ralph-Sheila" or "Dinner RS-SS" instead.

Meeting agenda. Always include the purpose, agenda, and desired outcomes for meetings you arrange. This may be the second trickiest part of setting up a meeting, particularly if others have more influence on the agenda than you do. Try to get as clear as you can about the purpose and desired outcomes before you start arranging the meeting. If you are not in charge of the meeting, try to get information on purpose, outcomes, and a draft agenda from the person that is. If that is a struggle, *propose something* to the person in charge of the meeting. They will let you know if they agree. It is often easier for a busy senior leader to respond to a proposal than to create it on their own.

Providing an agenda is essential for attendees to prepare for the meeting. Sending a meeting agenda is just a way to execute the PAASTUB process starting with Step 1 Purpose Clear. The agenda is your outline of the steps it takes to get from the start of the meeting to the desired outcomes. If your thinking about the agenda is unclear when you send the announcement or request, just include a draft of some quick ideas for the agenda and solicit input from prospective attendees. Your attendees will help you get clarity.

Meeting location. If the meeting is in a room or building where you work, identify the precise location in the email or meeting request. When you are setting up a call with just one person, use the meeting location field to enter who initiates the call and what number to use (e.g., "Ralph calls Don, 555-1212"). If the meeting is a conference call where everyone dials the same number to join, just enter that number and the meeting passcode.

Use RSVP correctly. RSVP is an abbreviation of the French command, *répondez s'il vous plaît*. It is frequently misused in meeting invitations. To use RSVP correctly requires that you understand what it actually means. Many senders either don't know what RSVP means or don't think recipients do. I frequently see it used inappropriately in constructions such as "If you plan to attend, RSVP to ..." In French, RSVP means "please reply" not "reply if you please," or "reply if you plan to attend." It is a command, not a request, so you should think of it as an order to "reply no matter what."

When is it appropriate to order people to reply to your invitation? When you need to know how many people are coming or you have specific assignments for the people that are coming. You need to know how many people are coming if seating is limited, you are providing refreshments, or there is some minimum number of required attendees to make the event practical.

"Save the date." This kind of meeting invitation subject sets my teeth on edge. Never, never (am I being clear enough?) send a meeting or event announcement with "save the date" in the subject. "Save the date" in the subject is just a waste of valuable space. Those characters tell recipients *nothing useful*. From reading Chapter 6, Subject as Art, the importance and benefit of brief, concise subjects with keywords should be clear. "Save the date" is like a keyword, but it is *too long*. For meeting emails, begin the subject with "meeting" ("mtg" is better) and follow that text with the day, time, and subject of the meeting. All "save the date" communicates is that sender is announcing an event. What would that be? A recipient cannot know why until they open the message. An Email Ninja <u>never</u> makes their recipients work that hard.

In the next section, I describe tactics that improve meeting notifications.

There are two good ways to announce meetings, each with advantages, limitations, and strategies for doing it well. The first way is to create the meeting on your own electronic calendar and send an invitation to attendees. The second is to send an email with the meeting details in the body of the email. In both cases, use a subject that identifies the meeting topic, date, time, and location.

Calendar program meeting invitations. If you use a calendar program to manage your time commitments, enter the meeting there after you have set the day and time of the meeting. All calendar applications allow you to send invitations via email. Make sure you enter the agenda and desired outcome of the meeting in the notes field of the event.

The advantages of sending meeting invitations through your calendar program are the application composes the emails for you and it keeps track of who has accepted the invitation. Simple, right?

There are three disadvantages of sending calendar-based meeting invitations. The first is that some desired participants may not use a calendar program to manage their schedules. They may not be able to use the information sent in a meeting request. In this case, you have to send them email notifications, which I discuss below. Second, every time you make an edit to the meeting notes, such as a minor change to the agenda, meeting invitees will get a new notification without explanation, which can be confusing. Unlike the "track changes" mode in word processors, calendar programs don't identify for meeting invitees what you changed. They just send another invitation email. So much for Automated Intelligence ruling the world. For this reason, you should explain what is new at the top of the meeting notes field whenever you make changes.

Third, it can be cumbersome to use calendar-based invitations when you are notifying a large number of people about an event. A meeting *announcement* is better for this. For meeting announcements, attendance is often optional and you don't have to deal with a mountain of email accept or decline replies.

All laptop and desktop calendar applications and most mobile devices can send iCal or vCal attachments via email message. This is the best approach if you don't know which application recipients use.

iCal and vCal attachments contain all the meeting details and notes and are recognized by nearly all calendar apps. In the body of the email you send, you should still use a BLUF to explain the basics of the meeting (location, date, subject) and how to use the calendar attachment. Forwarding Cal attachments is the best way to avoid inbox clutter from a large number of replies. You can do an internet search to learn how to do this for your calendar program (search term: [Program name] forwarding meetings via email).

Email meeting announcements. This is a normal email that has all the details of the meeting in text form. When you send an email meeting notification, use the PAASTUB process for composing the message. You should provide the meeting details in the following order:

- BLUF (answers what is this about?, what is the action?, and why is this important?)
- Date
- Time
- Meeting Title
- Location
- Agenda or Brief Summary of Meeting

The BLUF of the message invitation for the event should begin with a single sentence describing the meeting or event ("What is this about?"). The date, time, and location should already be in the subject, but should be repeated either in the BLUF or directly below. The second sentence of the BLUF should describe generally who needs to attend and why ("What is the action?"). Don't list every single person if the meeting has many attendees. The third sentence describes the desired outcome and significance ("Why is this important?"). If you don't include an agenda in the first meeting email, inform recipients that you will provide one via separate correspondence at a later, specific date.

The next two sections describe how to improve emails dealing with action.

Taking Action

Taking action is doing what was requested of you or providing information. The key elements for taking action well are: collecting all the actions requested in an email, understanding what is expected of you, and using a system to manage the actions that others request. This section suggests some tactics for each key element.

Be thorough. If a sender has asked you to provide something, answers to questions, comments, a file, etc., be sure to provide everything they requested in your reply, if possible. Unless you have trained them or given them a copy of this book, be prepared for actions scattered throughout their email. When actions *are* scattered, collect what you can from a quick scan, put them at the top of your reply, and precede them with text like "This is the list of actions I think you requested. Did I capture everything?" and answer each one. The "did I capture everything" statement is an indicator that you want their help to make sure you left nothing out.   Later, face-to-face, you can give subordinates feedback about the need to group all actions together after the BLUF as described in the previous section. If you cannot provide everything requested right away, send what you can with a note that more is coming and an estimate of when you will send it.

Some people like answering questions "inline" in the originator's email. This means that you type your text amongst theirs, in a different color if possible, in the copy of their original email that is almost always included with replies. I think this is a bad practice for several reasons. First, it can get confusing for the reader if they buried their questions within a paragraph somewhere in the middle of their email. While this is a bad practice on their part, trying to insert your answers in the middle of a long email just compounds the problem because it requires lots of scrolling to find your responses. Second, you often won't know how their email client is set up. Unless their email client supports HTML text, they won't be able to see your colored text so it will be a challenge for them to distinguish your text from theirs. This is why it is better to extract their questions and put them at the top of your reply.

It is a hallmark of professionalism and effectiveness to answer all questions from someone's email. This may require that you read the original email several times to find questions scattered like confetti. See Chapter 11, Collect Actions, for the tactics you should use in your own emails. If you cannot answer all their questions, be clear about when you can or what the obstacles are.

Get clarity. If you think there is any ambiguity in the action requested by someone, reply immediately and clear it up. Recall that an action specifies who does what by when. If the sender does not provide all of these elements, ask. I never accept action requests without knowing what the need date is. If the action is complicated or has multiple parts, paraphrase it to reflect your understanding and use a quick reply to check that understanding with the requesting party.

Managing actions. This is going to get a little bit geeky so brace yourself. I don't believe you can manage the tsunami of actions that come your way daily through email and text without some kind of system. This section briefly describes the really simple system I use for managing actions.

The email inbox metaphor is only superficially useful and definitely breaks down when it comes to managing emailed actions. An email inbox lacks the real affordances of a physical inbox and paper. "Affordance" refers the relationship between an actor and a physical object that permit action (Gibson, 1977, 1979; Norman, 2013). The design of a physical inbox allows a person to remove things, physically change them (e.g., writing notes, fastening to other things), and manipulate them (e.g., throw them away or collect them in a folder with other material). An email inbox supports none of these actions so it is more like a store window display. I note this because email in general and virtual inboxes in particular are terrible for managing actions, particularly complex ones. I use Evernote to manage the actions that I get in email. There are many software tools for this and you can also use a notebook, word processor file, or spreadsheet. Evernote works well enough for me, but may not be available on all office systems. The primary reason I use Evernote is it allows me to forward emails to my Evernote "inbox." From there, I can easily change and manipulate the text to integrate email actions with my existing task management system.

I am not in search of an optimal solution for task management, just one I understand and works "well enough." I recognize that "well enough" is very subjective and there are numerous books you can read on task management. My system is based on David Allen's Getting Things Done (2015), which I encourage you to consult and adapt for your own needs just like I did. The next section provides examples of the most important tactics I use to request action from others.

Tactics for Assigning Action

Some of the material in this section is repeated from Chapter 4, which describes Step 2 of the PAASTUB process, Action. I repeated it because it is really important and you don't have to flip back to Chapter 4. What's new is that the tactics below for conveying action are integrated with other steps in the PAASTUB process so you get the best results when assigning action.

Anatomy of good action. Use the "Action" keyword in the subject and make a brief statement of the action the second sentence of the BLUF. Action comes right after "what is this about?" for simple actions you assign to one person. Recall that the three components of a good action statement are: *who* does *what* by *when*.

- **Who has the action?** When you send an action request to just one person, you might think the *who* would be obvious, but why take a chance? Even in this case, the best practice is to start the second sentence of the BLUF with "I need you to ..." to be as clear as possible. Sometimes, it is necessary to send email for a project where individual members of a group have different actions. In this case, the second sentence of the BLUF should be "There are actions for Bob, Mary, and Griselda in this email" or "Actions for Bob, Mary, and Griselda needed by 5 Sept." Calling out action parties by name really gets their attention. Doing so right after a sentence identifying what the message is about makes it likely they will see the word "action" and their name in the preview of the message.
- **What is the action?** The list of all actions and responsible parties follows the BLUF. Good action statements use simple and concrete language. Action statements are no place to show off your impressive vocabulary. Instead of "contact Mr. Smith about the meeting" use "Get meeting details (time, date, location, desired outcomes) from Mr. Smith." Instead of "take the lead on the event risk assessment for our next planning call" use "run a ten-minute risk assessment on our next planning call. Solicit risk inputs from others before the call. For each risk: explain what it is, why it is a risk, and how it can be mitigated." Instead of "provide feedback on the document" use "provide comments and feedback on the document, focusing specifically on feasibility of the proposal, steps in the action

plan, and anything you think is missing."

- **When the action is needed.** Every action you request *must* have a due date. If you can, explain why you chose the due date ("so I can submit my application for X"). Due dates are essential for recipients to decide if they can accomplish the action. They are also related to the reminder you are going to send if the action is late. Even if you think the need date is "whenever," *make one up*. It must be defensible because you might get challenged. The first two questions an action recipient is likely to ask himself or herself are: 1) Do I have the ability to do this? and 2) Do I have time to complete it by the due date given all the other things I have going on? Even if they have the ability to do the action, they may not have the time. You want to know that as soon as possible. Most busy people prioritize their actions by due dates. Providing an action due date in the request simplifies their analysis. If you don't provide due date, you are leaving it up to recipients to decide when it is due. This could be bad for two reasons. First, their idea of a reasonable completion date may not match yours. Second, it is likely that *both of you* will forget about the action. Without an action due date, it is awkward to send a followup. If you never provided a due date, how could the action be late?

Collect actions after the BLUF. For all action emails with more than one action, group all the actions and questions right after the BLUF. Use a heading like "ACTION SUMMARY" that is easy for readers to scan. Even if it makes sense to embed actions with context in the body of the email, collect them after the BLUF. Putting all the actions and questions in one place makes it unlikely that readers will leave any out when they reply. Put each action, action party, and due date on a separate line. Precede each item in this summary with "Q1" or "A1," etc.

Make action as easy as possible. The first step in making actions easier for readers is to use simple, concrete language to describe the action ("I need you to do X"). The second step is to provide all the resources needed to take the action. If you want someone to review something (a file, email you sent previously, or web page), include a copy of the file, text, or link with the action email. Don't make them search for it. If you want them to call someone, include the phone number, if you know it. If you want them to send an email, provide a draft, which was recommended in Chapter 10.

Broadcast actions. Broadcast actions are not directed to a specific individual or small group, but rather everyone in the organization. Broadcasting actions to an entire organization may be necessary periodically. Examples include hurricane preparations or taking a quality of life survey. Some ways of broadcasting actions work better than others. An ineffective way is to send lots of reminder emails begging people to take the action because it is either hard or impossible (anonymous quality of life surveys) to track individual completion. The reminder emails seldom get laggards to finish and just annoys the people that have have. The best way to manage broadcast actions is to use the organizational hierarchy. In most organizations, everyone reports to *someone*. A good broadcast action email should have three sub-actions. First is to take the survey, for example. Second is to report completion to a supervisor. Third is for supervisors to provide a status by a date like the end of the week. If the action is optional, modify the second action to report "no interest" and modify the third action to report status anonymously or something similar. Followup reminder emails can then be targeted at just those supervisors that have not reported 100% completion of the action, which avoids irritating the entire organization. People seem to take actions much more seriously if they know someone is keeping track (shocking, but true). This is particularly true if the person keeping track is their supervisor.

Information only emails. Even if you are just providing a link with a full explanation or unsolicited information, you are still requesting that the recipients follow the link or consider using the information. If you provide information and don't expect a reply, use the "info" keyword in the subject and make this clear in the first sentence of your BLUF. Readers will be alerted by "info" that they don't even have to open the email. They still might do so if you use a particularly creative subject, which should always be your goal. The next section illustrates the important points of this chapter with examples.

Note: many of the examples include suggested subjects to accompany the text. This is to help readers get accustomed to the idea of subjects being inseparable from the body of the email.

Examples

Update Subjects (new text goes at the beginning of subjects)

In the original email, the sender asked if we were still going to have a call about a meeting we were both attending.

Original Subject: Some ideas and lessons to prep for the meeting
Updated Subject: Yes, still talking-[original subject here]

In the original email, the sender asked if I could supply comments for posting on Twitter

Original Subject: Re: Bob Skype
Updated Subject: Can supply twitter comments-Bob Skype

In the original email, the sender wanted to know if I could be the meeting leader because he would be late

Original Subject: At risk: E22
Updated Subject: Ready to lead: At risk: E22

In the original email, the sender wanted comments on a proposed travel itinerary

Original Subject: October
Updated Subject: Thoughts re: 17-24 Oct itinerary

In the original email, the sender provided an email link for a video. I couldn't watch it because the link didn't work.

Original Subject -> Your guitar
Updated Subject: Uh oh: can't view-Your guitar

In the original email, the sender was writing to express concern about medical notes I sent that had been forwarded to her.

Original Subject: Fwd: Re: Ralph's Medical Notes
Updated Subject: Concerned re Ralph's condition

Write about others cautiously

What you want to write -> I can't get Bob to return my emails.

What you should write -> I have not heard back from Bob via email. I will follow up by phone or see him in person. (All you know for sure is that Bob has not replied. There could be many benign reasons for this. Stick to the facts instead of implying that Bob is intentionally not replying to you.)

What you want to write -> I have never seen a conference this poorly organized.

What you should write -> I am struggling to register and use the website to plan for my conference attendance. (It really doesn't matter what you think about the conference organization. These are the problems you are having.)

Don't forward criticism

If someone sends text like this -> Pete doesn't know what he's talking about.

Revise it thusly -> Pete [has some concerns about the project that we need to address.] (When someone sends an email to me with this original text about Pete, I replace it with something much less critical and place the new text in brackets. Pete could read the revised text and not get upset and putting the revised text in brackets sends a strong signal to the originator. Later I can give face-to-face feedback to the originator.)

If someone sends text like this -> The operation was a fiasco and the planners were idiots.

Revise it thusly -> The operation [had some difficulties] and the planners [may have lacked experience or resources, but it is hard for me to know.]

Explain forwarded messages

Original email -> A colleague sent me an email with some links explaining the value of creating "storyboards" for presentations. This is how I passed it on to others.

Updated subject -> The value of storyboards

BLUF to accompany the forwarded email -> Below is an interesting note about "storyboarding" presentations. It includes an example and links to two really good Ted Talks. I thought of you when I read the words "making a video or an event whose purpose is to change an attitude or tell a memorable story."

Summarize attachments

- Sample Explanation 1 -> Enclosed are two program PDF's. One is a flyer for the two-day conference ("Program leaflet 2 days"). The other is a flyer for the one-day conference for newcomers ("Program leaflet preconference").
- Sample Explanation 2 -> Attached is the summary of the report's six principles that may be relevant for your upcoming offsite.
- Sample Explanation 3 -> The first file contains the core elements of the book in one paragraph (how's that for concise?) with an example, two pages (file name begins with "Book Summary").
- Sample Explanation 4 -> Proposal Defense Prep Guidance.docx -> this is the file my Chair sends to help students prepare, it was wonderful. It can help you too.

Don't recall

Instead of trying to recall the email, send a correction with clear subject and BLUF like this:

Subject: **correction** meeting is *2* Dec, 2pm (the asterisks make it clear what you are correcting)

BLUF: I had the wrong time for the meeting in the prior email. Please disregard that email.

Meeting date and time

Meeting Scheduling (time and date unknown, depending on others' availability)

Example 1->Many participants, availability known

Subj: Alert:-proposed (event title) dates 7-8 Nov, 29 Nov

BLUF: I propose two options for the call: 7-8 Nov (date depends on your time zone) or 29 Nov. My proposal is to use 8/7 Nov as the primary date and save 29 Nov as the backup. Let me know what you think by 1 Nov.

* Option 1: 0700 in Sydney on 8 Nov (Raul) is 7 Nov for everyone else, 2100 GMT (Bruce and Sheila), 1600 GMT-5 (Buffy and Timmy), and 1400 GMT-7 (Ralph). This avoids my conflict with 8-11 Nov.
* Option 2: 2300 in Sydney on 29 Nov (Raul), same day for all, is 1300 GMT (Bruce and Sheila), 0800 GMT-5 (Buffy and Timmy), and 0600 GMT-7 (Ralph). This is the only way to match (Raúl's) last available day before travel and not conflict with Thanksgiving weekend in the US and match (Buffy's) availability.

Call Summary: The purpose of the call is to discuss the team's progress on solving world hunger. A more detailed agenda will be provided after we decide on the day and time of the call.

Example 2->Two participants, availability unknown
Subj: talk Fri or next week?

Email text: I am available tomorrow, Friday, just about any time after 1000 your time except for 15-1600.
Next week
Mon or Tues any time after 1000.
Wed 11-1800
After Wed, things get much trickier (how far you go into the future depends on many variables, my rule of thumb is no more than a week)

Requesting availability
Subject -> Quick-When avail 3-15 Dec, 1hr call re Proj Plan? (49 characters)
Subject -> Action-Avail dates 3-15 Dec, Proj Plan call (43 characters)

All Meeting Emails
Example meeting invitation (a phone call to support a podcast recording)

Subject: Episode 12-Intro 29 Nov

BLUF: The recording introduces the new podcasters to the listeners with the current podcasters functioning like guides and welcomers. Duration is less than an hour.

Event title: Episode 12-Introduction

Date: 29 November (repeat the date, some people don't look at subjects closely)

Time: 20:00 GMT (useful for meetings with participants in different time zones)

or

Time: 0700 in Sydney (Amy), 2100 GMT (Raul and Sheila), 1600 GMT-5 (Spike and Cassius), and 1400 GMT-7 (Ted) (listing the time and timezone for each participant is much clearer and participants will be able to catch any errors you make)

Location: Skype call for podcast recording

Agenda:

(Proposed, please provide recommendations)

- Individual introductions (just names and locations)
- Short statement about the podcast-(Ted)
- Extended introductions and backgrounds of new guest hosts that could cover things like: degree, research interests, current position and research activities

All the necessary information for pasting into a calendar event is included: Subject (same as meeting title), BLUF, Date, Meeting Title, Time, Location, Agenda or Brief Summary.

Example meeting announcement (a phone call to support a podcast recording)

Subject: Email productivity tips 29 Jan 1p Auditorium (year is omitted because it is usually obvious and time is abbreviated, both to keep subject shorter)

BLUF: 1 hour talk by email productivity expert Dr. Ralph Soule. Dr. Soule will introduce the email composition and management system from his book. Q&A at end. (Keep it brief)

Event title: Email Productivity Tips

Date: 29 Jan (repeat date)

Time: 1 pm

Location: Auditorium

Attendance: Space is limited to the first 100 responders since the auditorium seating is limited. Inform Bob Soule (x-1982, bsoule@notarealaddress.com) if you plan to attend. (Use this text if it is important to keep track of who is coming or to manage attendance if seating or participation is limited. You can also provide a web link to a system that manages attendees and notifications.)

Summary: Dr. Soule will provide an overview of his book and discuss the principles he uses to improve his communications productivity and effectiveness. There will be time for questions. Dr. Soule will be available to sign copies of his book at the end of the presentation. (Use Summary in lieu of a more detailed agenda, when appropriate. More details can be provided, as desired. Note that the details come at the bottom, not the top of the email.)

Requesting Action (Be clear about who does what by when)

Example 1 -> Information only, no action expected
Subject: Info-recipe for chicken soup
BLUF: I have provided a chicken soup recipe, no response needed.

Example 2 -> Action needed
Subject: Need approval of travel 12 Dec, pls (Action stated very briefly in subject with "need" as the first word. This is a gentle way of requesting action for superiors and people you don't know well.)
BLUF: Debbie entered my travel request for another trip. Soon it will come into your approval queue. Pls approve by 12 Dec.

Example 3 -> Action needed
Subject: Need info re days to attend 2-5 Feb conf
BLUF: Do you have insight on what events are worth attending at the conference in Feb? I may be able to attend, but it is not clear which days I should attend or when the panel session is. I need to know before 1 Jan to make travel plans. (The question you need answered is the first sentence of the BLUF.)

(Background information) While it seems a bit pricey to fly from Albuquerque for just one day and a chance to speak for a few minutes, it might be worthwhile if there are things worth attending over two or more days. I had trouble figuring this out from the conference program so that is why I am asking for your help.

Example 4 -> Action needed

Subject: Need help-info on Lac-Mégantic disaster?

BLUF: Since you two presented a mini-case study on the event at the Apr conference, could you tell me what sources were particularly useful? I might use the Lac-Mégantic disaster to illustrate some of my points. I am preparing a presentation for the 2017 safety conference. Can you reply by 2 Feb? (The BLUF is all you need in an action request like this.)

Example 5 -> Action needed

Subject: (5 Dec) need input-Ralph's blog post plans, suggestions (Project actions sent to specific people in one email.)

BLUF: I seek input on my blog post plan by 5 Dec. Before Christmas, I will send deliverables for the first set of blog posts. By Friday you can expect two drafts of posts for Jan. Other actions noted below.

Action Summary

A) (Ralph) Is planning and 2 blogposts drafts by Friday ok?

B) (Sheila, Ralph)Would you like posts on current issues from an Organizational Science perspective (suggestion 1)?

C) (Sheila, 10 Dec) Can you can meet to discuss interviewing some co-workers (e.g., organizational designers) (suggestion 2)?

(Background information can follow.)

Note that all actions are grouped after the BLUF

Taking action

Example 1 -> providing feedback on attachments

Subject: Done-comment on draft by 3 Dec

BLUF: I embedded many comments and suggested edits in the attached document. I am available to discuss any that are not clear. Below is a summary of the most significant comments I made.

Comment Summary

* The term "sustain" is used in several places in a way that does not appear consistent with the book. I cannot tell if that was a small error or is based on a deeper misunderstanding of the concept.

* There are many local projects identified, but it is not clear how they are being used to develop personnel. I think the document could be

improved by being more explicit about that.

* There are lots of activities identified on pages 2-4, but the implementation plan is weak on how, *exactly*, they will be mapped to the strategic priorities. I cannot tell what people will be learning otherwise.

(You should never write, "see comments in attachment" because that requires the recipient to open the attachment and study it in detail to even get a brief idea of what you wrote. Make it clear in the body of the email, right below the BLUF, what you think the most important comments are.)

Example 2
Original Subject: (5 Dec) need input-Ralph's blog post plans, suggestions
Revised Subject: Bob's input-Ralph's blog post plans, suggestions

(Don't default to "Re: (5 Dec) need input-Ralph's blog post plans, suggestions" because it is ambiguous. It could be the input or could be questions. Replacing "Re" with "Bob's input" makes it clear from scanning the inbox what the email is about. Don't use "Re: (5 Dec) ..." even if you are asking a question. Replace "Re:" with "question-". This looks much more compelling in a person's inbox.)

BLUF: Here's input to one of my two actions. I will provide the second action by Friday.

Example 3
Revised Subject: Ralph Soule conf data
BLUF: I copied the questions from the email and provided my answers below.

Name: Dr. Ralph Soule
Organization: None
Title: Independent Researcher
Address: (inserted here)
Reason for Attending: Interest in email productivity
Meal pref: Beef

Example 4 Quick reply
Subj: Will review proposals soon

BLUF: I noted between flights that both of you provided proposals to review. I plan to give feedback soon, but it may not be until this weekend.

Example 5 Quick reply
Subj: Ralph behind, will review doc early Sun (No body text is needed in an email like this, particularly if you keep the text from the original document in the body of the email. If you do reply to the email asking for action, replace the "Re:" default subject with something like this one.)

Key points from Chapter 11

- Nearly all email falls into one of four types: invitations, announcements, taking action, and requesting action. This chapter identified tactics for being more effective with each category.
- The philosophy behind all the email tactics in this chapter is: don't make recipients work harder than necessary or force them to solve study problems that you created.
- When someone sends you an email with an ambiguous, vague subject, "fix" it when you reply. Improving poor email subjects demonstrates your grasp of the message content, makes it easier to search for the message later, and gently nudges the sender toward better email subjects in the future.
- Update subjects frequently. If the topic changes, which it often does after the second email, update the subject. This is particularly important for emails that begin with a keyword indicating high priority like URGENT or HOT. As soon as the email is no longer a high priority, remove high priority keywords.
- Write about others cautiously. Whenever you mention a third party in email, write as if they were going to read it. Emails have an alarming tendency to end up in the inbox of the people you wrote badly about. The best approach is to copy anyone you write about to ensure you don't misrepresent their views. Edit any strong criticism from others before you send your message.
- Criticize gently. This is sound advice in general, but particularly important in email messages. Email criticism

comes across much harsher than face to face.

- Make humor explicit. Adding (smile) or (joke) after an ironic or slightly sarcastic statement is great insurance against people misinterpreting what you intended to be funny.

- Be cautious with Bc. Don't use Blind copy (Bc) as a way to keep others informed secretly. It is more professional to forward the original message with the Info keyword to the person you want to inform. Include a brief explanation of why you think they need to be informed.

- Explain forwarded messages. Don't assume it is obvious to others why you forwarded something. Adding "FYI" is not sufficient. Two or three sentences beginning with "Forwarded because" are usually adequate.

- Summarize every attachment. Don't make recipients open attachments to understand your reason for including them. That is a study problem. List each filename and why you think its contents will be useful to the recipients.

- Single topic per message. Using a single topic per email makes it easier for recipients to manage their actions. This is particularly helpful when there are actions related to different topics or have different due dates.

- Use whitespace to improve readability. Don't dump all your text into one long paragraph. Blank lines and whitespace make it easier to read longer emails. Keep formatting simple.

- Drop "dear all." This just wastes space. Get right to the point by starting with the BLUF. The BLUF is what the recipients care the most about. The salutation "Dear" anybody is so old school.

- Keep signatures short. Keep your signature short and use an abbreviated signature for replies. Long signatures can be ignored at the bottom of single emails, but they are tedious when you have replied several times in a series of emails.

- Get permission for large attachments. Seek permission to send files bigger than 5MB. You don't want your email to be responsible for shutting down someone's mailbox.

- Don't recall messages. Recalling messages is a waste of time and can be confusing. It is better to send a correction email with a subject beginning with "Correction-(what is being fixed)" and some brief text explaining the correction.

- Don't send SPAM. Don't waste other people's time by sending them SPAM in the form of chain letters, unexplained links, and jokes. Do you really want to be responsible for melting someone else's computer? Save that content for social media. Always explain business-related links lest they look like SPAM or phishing attempts.

- Learn to search well. Avoid complex folder management systems for email and learn to search well. Modifying email subjects to make them very specific and clear really helps search efficiency. Save any attachments you want to keep in your normal location for files.
- Do a final review before sending. The final review is an important and really useful part of sending good email. Use it to focus on what the reader a) needs to take your action or b) asked you to provide. The final review is what separates an Email Ninja from an Email Doofus.
- Never ask for someone to meet or call you without telling them when you will be available.
- Provide an agenda in advance of any meeting. This applies even if the meeting with just with one other person.
- Use RSVP correctly. Remember that it means "respond no matter what." Don't look silly by writing "RSVP if you plan to attend."
- Send meeting requests to required participants. Meeting requests make it easy to add the event to their calendar if they keep their calendar electronically.
- If you seek action from someone or a group, include all the components of an effective action: who does what by when. Always include your due date in the subject and the BLUF. Summarize the action in the second sentence of the BLUF and group all actions in more detail for each right after the BLUF. If different recipients have actions in an email, make it clear in the list of actions who is responsible for each.
- Broadcast actions are applicable to everyone in the organization. Manage them through the organizational hierarchy. This enables you to task the supervisors to keep track of who has completed the action and eliminates the need to send nagging reminder emails.
- If you think the action assigned to you is unclear, get clarity right away. Ask the sender. Never accept an action unless you are clear what is expected by when.

- Use some kind of tool outside of your email inbox to manage your actions. If you have more than a few actions, your email inbox is the wrong tool for managing them.
- Be thorough about taking requested actions. If actions are scattered throughout an email you receive, read the email carefully to make sure you found them all and check with the sender to be sure, when appropriate. Put the actions right after the BLUF in your reply.

Part 3 of the book provides templates and tools based on the email system described in Part 1 and the strategies and tactics of Part 2. They are designed to help you put the system in action.

Part 3 - Email Ninja Tools

BLUF: This part of the book provides templates and tools based on the email system of Part 1 and the email strategies and tactics of Part 2. I encourage you to adapt the tools to your specific situation so they meet the needs of the work you do and the emails you send most often.

Chapter 12: Tools

BLUF: The tools and templates in this chapter make it easy to get started using my system for more effective email. Research suggests that this is particularly helpful for learning new behaviors (Haidt, 2012; Heath & Heath, 2011). This chapter provides four tools for reference (Email Ninja checklist, sample subject keywords, final message review checklist, and email etiquette guide) and four templates for recurring emails (poor subject reminders, teaching people about BLUFs, event arrangement, and event announcement).

Introduction

The tools and templates of this chapter will help you become more productive right away. In time, you will internalize the system, making your email communications much more effective. I think of tools as things to help you do things and provide leverage. Templates are models to copy for emails you send frequently. Follow the models, develop your own, and soon the practices will become second nature. Practice makes all the difference for becoming an Email Ninja.

There are four tools in this chapter that will help you produce more effective email. The first tool is the Email Ninja checklist, arranged with the PAASTUB acronym for ease of recall. Like a paystub, you should think of the Email Ninja checklist as the "payoff" you will gain from using the system in this book. The second tool is the list of subject keywords that I find most useful for telegraphing the purpose of emails. The third tool is a final, after composition but before pressing "send," email message review checklist.

The fourth high-leverage tool is an email etiquette guide. I wrote the guide so you can use it "as is" or customize it for your organization and its norms.While every organization will have different specific needs for email etiquette guidance, the guide is a really good place to start. I have used it at several organizations to clearly and succinctly convey guidelines for effective email communication. The email etiquette guide can provide leverage in your organization or work group in two ways.

First, the expectations fill a gap that exists in the email training done by many organizations. Organizational email training tends to focus on the technical aspects of using email programs, not on communicating well. The email etiquette guide is a set of basic guidelines that bridge the gap between software skill and communications effectiveness. For some people, this is not so much a gap as a chasm.

Second, the guide can serve as a standard for coaching performance improvement. You can refer people to it when they veer (and they certainly will) from the effective communications path you prefer. These people are easy to identify because they will continue sending messages with single-word subjects like "meeting" even after reading this book. If you are a manager, you can use the guide close the gap between the emails these people send and the type you *need* them to send.

This chapter has four templates for emails that recur frequently: giving email subject guidance to someone that desperately needs it, explaining what the Bottom Line Up Front is, arranging meeting date and time, and announcing events. You should keep the templates in your drafts folder so you can copy and paste from them quickly. The four templates may also give you ideas for additional templates for your own circumstances.

The PAASTUB Checklist

Print this page and keep it near your computer. The PAASTUB steps are:

- **(P)urpose clear**. Know the category of your email before you start writing the message. Everything you write must support your purpose. Recall that most email falls into four types:
    - Announcing or inviting people to a meeting
    - Setting up a meeting with actions and agendas
    - Action or information needed from someone
    - Giving information without action
- **(A)ction**. What do you need done? Who has the action? When do you want it? If you are providing something, what is it? Briefly state these in the BLUF and provide necessary details in the message body. If there is more than one action, collect all of them after the BLUF.
- **(A)udience**. Who needs to receive your email to accomplish your purpose? DO NOT reply to all. Who will change what they are doing based on what you write? Include people on Cc: if they have TOLD you to do so. If you add new addressees, include text to explain what the message is about and why it should matter to them.
- **(S)ubject as Art**. Make the subject of your email eye catching and compelling. Use humor and irony whenever possible because they attract attention. Make the purpose of your email clear **from** *the subject line alone*. Use keywords like Action and Info. Make the length about 25-30 characters.
- **(T)ake Out the Trash**. Remove anything that is not part of what you *choose* to communicate like lengthy signatures, disclaimers, warnings, and email addresses from prior forwards. Leave *nothing* to distract people from getting the information they need quickly.
- **(U)gly Remarks Edited**. Don't pass on harsh language or strong criticism from others. Edit or delete it before sending. If you write about someone, include them on distribution. Imagine them reading what you or someone else wrote about them.
- **(B)LUF**. Review the BLUF to be sure it aligns with the purpose

of the message, the content, and the subject you used. Adjust the subject, BLUF, and text as necessary after you finish composing. The first sentence of the BLUF is what the email is about. The second sentence describes the action. The third sentence explains why the issue is important. The BLUF is a blend of brevity and laser-like clarity. While the BLUF could be just one sentence, it should not exceed four sentences or three lines of text.

Subject Keywords

Email subject keywords are useful shorthand that get people's attention and telegraph the content of the email. All subjects should begin with a keyword followed by a dash and additional text that makes the content of the email clear.

Examples of useful email subject keywords:

- Alert (big problem, read right away)
- HOT (very important, better than URGENT because it is shorter, but don't overuse)
- Problem (but not a big problem). An alternative, more humorous version is "Uh-oh" (see below). Both "problem" and "uh-oh" are better than "PLEASE READ" or "Important" because they are shorter. For big problems, you could use Alert, HOT, or Big Prob
- Ouch (something unexpected or difficult)
- Action (you want the recipient to do something based on the email). Always include a due date in the subject of an "action" email like "(due 1-18) Action-provide comments on plan".
- Need Help (a more gentle way to request action, use with superiors or people you don't know well)
- Question (makes it clear you need something, more compelling and thus likely to get opened faster than "Re: (the old subject)")
- No fwd (for sending sensitive emails that requires special handling). "No fwd" is not a free pass to write disparaging things about others so use it sparingly. Always explain why you don't want the message forwarded at the top of the email

body.

- Update (new information for the reader and more compelling than "Re: [the old subject]")
- Reminder (when you have sent one email already, but received no response). Be gentle and polite when sending reminder emails to avoid really annoying the receiver and getting put into "ignore" mode.
- Mtg (for meeting details, include topic, date, time, location right in the subject). Call or Event are good alternatives such as "Call: 28 Jan 1p-Episode 30 recording"
- Info (no action, recipients should open only they have time or interest). They might not. Don't let it bother you.
- Late (to let someone know you are late responding)
- Long or Long msg (to warn your readers that it will take some time to read the message you are sending)

Email Final Review (before sending)

Re-read the email text, BLUF, and subject to answer these questions:

- Is the action statement (who, what, when) the first sentence of your BLUF?
- Is the action clear from the subject alone?
- Have you used punctuation and humor in your subject while keeping its length to about 30 characters? Even if you have no sense of humor, keep the subject short.
- Does the BLUF cover what the email is about, what the action is, and why it is important?
- Do you provide the action due date in both the subject and the BLUF?
- Are all the actions grouped immediately after the BLUF?
- Does the background material come after the description of the action?
- Is there sufficient background information after the actions to understand what needs to be done?
- Are the contents of all attachments summarized?
- Did you include as recipients all the people that need to know the contents or are mentioned in the message? Do you write

about anyone or any organization not represented on distribution (that would be bad)?

Sample Email Etiquette Guide

In this section, I provide a sample email etiquette guide that I used at several organizations. It is based on this book, but it is not a substitute for reading the book, of course. What kind of author would I be if I didn't believe that?

Only send the etiquette guide to the people if they work directly for you. As for your peers, you can't dictate how they write email, but you can suggest that reading it might be useful for them. Only send it if they ask. The advantage for an organization of issuing an email etiquette guide is that it provides a standard. Standards are helpful for teaching people when stray into bad email behavior. The guide is compact, making it easy to read in one sitting or during a conference call (not that I recommend do that). It is based on the system described in this book to help people be more effective with email. If you decide to use it, you should customize it for your organization.

Electronic Mail Etiquette

Summary: This document provides basic guidance for making your electronic mail (email) more effective for getting work done. It covers why email etiquette is important, an email philosophy, email productivity and composition tips, and some guidance on addressing (don't "reply to all"). The guidance is based on Ralph Soule's book, "Become an Email Ninja." If you follow this guidance, you will be a much more effective communicator, you will get yourself and others into trouble less frequently, and you will help others take action quicker.

Email Etiquette

Email is a fast, flexible, and powerful tool for getting things done. Email etiquette is a set of rules and behavioral conventions for what is appropriate practice in particular situations. Etiquette goes beyond "how to compose an email" and addresses **why** you should use email in particular ways. Etiquette also covers why email is not the right tool in certain situations.

Email is not perfect because it lacks the richness of face-to-face communications. Normal conversation oozes with subtle context, tone of voice, body language, and emotion that email cannot convey. It leaves a persistent record that you cannot control after you select "send." Crass mistakes and embarrassing gaffes in email live forever. The best reasons for following email etiquette are:

- Efficiency: emails that swiftly get to the point are much more effective than poorly worded emails. The same goes for attachments.
- Effectiveness: communication is only effective when appropriate information is written by the sender (hurdle #1) AND correctly perceived by the recipient (hurdle #2). Communication occurs in the mind of the recipient, not at the keyboard of the sender.
- Protection from misunderstandings: email has permanence and wide distribution that is at odds with its informal nature. You can get into a lot of trouble with "informal" communications like email. Miscommunication and damage to ones credibility and reputation are big risks. Poor email can result in lawsuits or be used out of context.
- Professionalism: by using proper email language, you will convey a professional image that reflects well on you and your organization.

Email Philosophy

When you're upset with someone, the last thing you should do is reply to their e-mail or speak negatively about them in an email addressed to someone else. Write every email as if the person or a member of the organization about which you are writing were reading it too. Seriously consider not writing anything derogatory about anyone. Beware that anything you write could be interpreted negatively or reflect badly on your organization, regardless of what you intended. If you feel you really must communicate something negative or sensitive, **stop writing an email and use the phone**. Do not use email to discuss sensitive information. If you don't want your email to be displayed on a bulletin board or quoted in the news media, **don't send it**. Never make any libelous, sexist or racially discriminating comments in emails, even if they are meant to be a joke.

Sometimes knowing when not to send an email is as important as deciding what to put in it. Use the "Two Email Rule." If you can't communicate your point or appear to be arguing with someone after two emails, stop ... sending ... emails ... Use the phone or go see the person to review the issue, figure out what's wrong, and reestablish your relationship.

Email is fast and convenient, but usually not for complex issues that involve subtlety and sensitive topics. Learn to recognize when it is more appropriate and easier to discuss such matters over the phone or in person. If someone else is having trouble making this distinction, send them a short reply like "I would be more comfortable talking about this over the phone or in person. Let's set that up. Here is when I will be available ..."

Try to respond to emails quickly, if possible. If this is not possible, send a short note to the sender stating that you received their message and expect to get back to them by a certain date. This is important because the sender may be waiting on your reply to take action. Fair or not, implicit in email is the assumption that response time is consistent with transmittal time (i.e., rapid).

Email Productivity

Do not forward non-work-related emails that others have forwarded to you. Spare your friends and co-workers and let them focus on work. Just because you find something funny or someone else forwarded something to you, don't compound the problem by sending it to even more people.

Meeting or Call Invitations

Avoid sending emails merely requesting a meeting or call. The boss gets to do this because he or she is the boss. Unless you are the boss, never send a message with "call me" or "let's meet" and leave it at that. The Outlook calendar provides two methods for arranging a meeting. The first is called a Meeting Request (method 1). The second is forwarding calendar items (method 2). If you do not know about these features of Outlook, learn about them or ask someone who does (faster). Both of these methods make it easy for others to add the meeting to their Outlook calendar and, with method 1, you can get a confirmation indicating whether the recipient can attend. Sometimes you want this when you need specific people to come to accomplish the meeting's purpose. When you are merely informing people about a meeting and their attendance is optional, use method 2. This involves creating the meeting on your own calendar, then forwarding the calendar item to others. People can add the details of the meeting to their calendar by just opening the icon they receive. If you inform many people of the meeting, you have saved each of them the time to copy and paste information on their own into their calendar. This is a wonderful time savings.

If you ask someone to call or meet with you, ALWAYS provide your availability in that email ("let's meet. I am available ...). This is method 3 for arranging meetings. Do this for several days in advance of the day you compose the email. The chances of randomly catching busy people at their desks and out of meetings in today's world are close to zero. If you provide your schedule information, the recipient's reply can set up the meeting. This is much more effective than "let's talk."

When you invite people to a meeting, make sure you clearly identify the day, time, location, purpose, preparatory material (read aheads), proposed agenda, and desired result from the meeting. **Never** send a message for a meeting that says, "see attached agenda" or "open flyer for details." Provide the important details in the body of the email so people don't have to waste time opening some huge file on their mobile devices. The subject of meeting invitations should contain the topic, date, time, and location. For example, "[Title] Mtg 10/2 1530 Conf Rm 1" so recipients can quickly see, without opening the email, that there is a meeting and when it is. Don't waste valuable subject space on meaningless expressions like "Save the date."

Email Composition

Your writing style says more about you than you realize. While e-mail might be viewed as an informal means of communication, your e-composition skills are a reflection on your knowledge and abilities. They also say something about your organization. Nobody cares about a few typos, but if you're consistently not capitalizing words that should be capitalized, using unconventional punctuation (i.e., putting

15 periods in a row instead of just three), spelling words incorrectly, and so on, you will come across as a person who does not know what he is doing. This will damage the confidence others have in you and your organization.

Keep your messages brief. If you can say it in three words, please . . . say it in three words. We are all busy and need to make best use of our time when writing and reading emails. Some of the attributes that support crisp (brief, clear) communications are:

· skillful and disciplined writing
· organized (outlines are your friend),
· on point, concise, brief, making the most of limited length,
· clearly expressed,
· actions clear.

Always use a super descriptive subject for your emails. What is "super descriptive?" It is a subject that makes it clear what is in your email from **the subject alone.** Sometimes, that's all people are going to read. People find it really annoying when someone sends messages with just "Hi" or "Meeting" in it. That tells no one anything useful. If you want action, say so (as in SUBJ: Action: [Topic]).

Brief keywords at the beginning of the subject are like emoticons for capturing attention and conveying the essence of what the message is about. Some examples are:

- Alert (big problem)
- HOT (very important, need real soon, similar to "Alert")
- Problem (but not a big problem)
- Need Help (for peers, people you don't know well or seniors)
- Action (to members of your team, makes it clear that the message has action for them)
- Question (possibly obvious, but makes it clear you need an answer, more compelling than "Re:")
- Due soon or Due [date] (conveys priority of an action item)
- Mtg [subj, date, time, location (if applicable)] (more useful than the odious "save the date")
- Correction (for correcting errors instead of recalling a prior message)

- Info (no action, read if time and interest permit, which might be never)
- Late (lets someone know you are late responding)
- Long or Long msg (warns readers that it will take some time to read the message you are sending)

Even worse (bordering on reprehensible) than a poorly constructed subject is using a "forward" or "reply" just to save starting a new message, changing the topic of the original email, and NOT changing the subject. Don't do this.

If you're going to forward a message to someone, strip all the extraneous information below your text before you send it. This includes: multiple lists of prior recipients in replies and forwards, "you will go to jail if I addressed my message improperly" disclaimers, privacy notices, and complicated email signatures. Most people have become so dependent on the "include copy of original" feature of email programs that this can take a little effort, but it makes an enormous difference in readability. Cleaning up messy email threads is just common e-courtesy. It is very difficult to make sense of an email that relies on understanding five or six previous emails, especially if none of them were originally sent to you. Summarize the issues raised by ALL the prior emails before sending to new recipients. "See below" is totally inadequate for helping people quickly understand the issue and necessary action. Do not send puzzles for your recipients to figure out.

"Spill the beans" early. Every message should begin with a BLUF (Bottom Line Up Front), which should be three, plus or minus one, sentences. The first sentence explains what your message is about (without the words "this message is about" if you can help it). Ex: "This message identifies strategies we should consider for achieving X by the deadline for project F." The second sentence explains what action you recommend or need by when. Ex: "Group Y should analyze the recommendations below, identify pros/cons, and choose a preferred approach by [date]. The third sentence explains why this is important (without using the words "this is important because"). Ex: "We must achieve X by the deadline or it will delay a series of other projects and lead to total protonic reversal [or similar calamity]." The first and third sentences can be swapped, if desired.

Many senior leaders are forced by the volume of email they receive to ruthlessly screen their email inboxes by BLUF. Outlook allows you to read about two lines of the BLUF as part of Auto Preview. Emails lacking a good subject and BLUF become a lower priority for opening. Put the details or background, if necessary, further down in the email or in attachments. Good headers for the text are: Bottom Line Up Front (BLUF) or Summary (including action desired), Urgency, Action, Background, and Discussion. If an extremely busy reader sees a message that contains several paragraphs without headers, they might miss something you want them to know.

Use one topic per message, if possible. Avoid combining unrelated topics in one email (unless they are really brief). Most people perform inbox "triage" by rapidly scanning one after another to find what is most important right now. Putting lots of topics, high and low priority, in the same email compounds the challenge of identifying importance. If you include several related topics in an email, use capitalized headings or paragraph numbers to help the person separate the topics. Stop to consider how the email will be received by someone that knows far less about the topic than you do. Really busy readers often don't have the time to study the entire message. Plan for this by staying focused on one topic and its important issues.

Make your email easy on the eyes. Use blank lines (hard carriage returns) to separate your paragraphs and headings. You may have to add one space to blank lines because some email systems remove lines that have no characters. Avoid using tabs because different e-mail programs can display tab stops differently. Use spaces if you need to indent something, but indenting the first line of each paragraph is unnecessary in email.

When replying to specific questions or issues raised by the sender, be sure to include a quotation from the original e-mail if you think it would be helpful. By default, all email programs include the full text of prior emails in replies, but that may not be sufficient if you want to address a particular sentence. Avoid replying on top of the text from the email you received. It is just too confusing to determine where their text ended and yours begins (even if you use ALL CAPS).

Attachments (documents, spreadsheets, etc.) are great . . . but don't abuse the concept. Mailing a simple 30K attachment is harmless, but when you need to send files larger than 5MB, ask the receiver's permission first. NOTE: Most government network administrators place restrictions on the size of messages users can receive. When someone sends a "large" attachment, the receiver may be locked out of his mailbox. If people are reading email on a mobile device, downloading large attachments takes a lot of time and they seldom display correctly. Do not send emails that require the reader to open an attachment to understand your key points or requested action. Explain every attachment you send or forward: name, content summary, and importance.

Readers don't want email messages with lots of fancy formatting and colors. Don't send messages in HTML or other special formats. Keep them basic and use plain text. Use asterisks to show *emphasis*. Indicate underlines _this_ way.

If you want action or help, make the deadline clear. Put it in the subject AND the BLUF.

If you need a senior executive to send an email on your behalf to get some action, always provide a draft of the email you want. Write it as if you were the person making the request. This will save them lots of time because you know exactly what the issue is and what action is necessary. Don't worry if you don't know *exactly* how they would write it. They will change what they need.

If you use abbreviations or acronyms, be sure your audience already knows what they stand for. The only way to be sure is spell them the first time in every email.

An email reply must answer all questions. Pre-empt further questions by being thorough. If you don't answer all the questions in the original email, you will receive further e-mails that will not only give you more work to do, but also irritate your reader by having to ask again. If you cannot answer all the questions at once, answer what you can and give an estimate for when you can answer the rest. If there are obstacles to providing answers, reply stating what those are. Thoroughness in your reply will impress readers with your efficient and thoughtful service, and it will reflect well on your organization.

Put your email signature on a budget. It should be no more than 2-3 lines (fewer if distribution of your email is to a group of people that already know you). Apart from the disclaimers your organization requires, your signature should only be your name, title, contact information, and URL. WORD can be set up to automatically attach a default signature file to the end of all your outgoing messages (including replies). They're perfect for conveying contact information, but keep them short and sweet. Spare the reader pithy quotes from Mother Teresa and Plato, please.

Before you send your message, take the time to do a final read. Spend extra time on the review if sending to a wide distribution or senior executives. Check for good alignment between the content of the message (usually only clear *after* you have written it), the subject, and the BLUF. Don't let actions and important information "sneak in" the message that are not reflected in the BLUF and subject. As long as your final review is longer than 30 seconds, you are likely to catch the biggest spelling, grammar, and "missing word" errors you made. Ask yourself, "Will the recipient understand the issue and just what I need them to do?" Make revisions until you are convinced they will.

Email Addressing

Use the Cc: (carbon copy) field sparingly. Try not to use Cc: unless the prospective recipient really needs to know what you are sending or it will be obvious to them why they are receiving the copy. What does "really needs to know" mean? It means the person will change something they are doing based on the information in the email. If not, don't include them "just because" they *might* want to know. They don't have time. Only include them if they have told you to do so.

Using the Cc: field can be confusing. Most readers scan messages looking for actions before they take the time to study who is To and who is Cc. If they see actions that don't apply to them, they will wonder why they were included. This is the tyranny of the Cc. You can easily add someone Cc: on a message and leave it up for them to figure out why you did it. In general, do not include the person in the Cc: field unless you have a specific reason for wanting them to see your message. Don't assume they will know. Make it clear: "I sent this message to the people on Cc: because ..." Instead of including someone Cc:, you can forward the message directly to them after you sent it. Include the reason why you did this.

Limit your use of "reply to all." "Reply to all" is often abused, particularly when people are debating something and there are many addressees. Few of them want the debate in their inboxes. Check the recipient list of the original email carefully before you "reply to all." Does everyone on the original distribution need to know whether you can attend a meeting, especially senior leaders? Hint: NO. **Rule of thumb**: don't "reply all" unless the sender asked for it.

Email Recalling and Delivery Receipts

Do not recall messages. Chances are that your message has already been delivered by the time you realize you made an error. A recall request is futile at that point. It is better to send an email with a statement that you made a mistake and supply the corrected information. Use the keyword "correction" in the subject. This is more efficient and less confusing than trying to recall your message.

Do not request delivery and read receipts. This annoys recipients before they even read your message. It usually does not work since the recipient could have blocked that function or his/her software might not support it. If someone refuses to read your emails, you have a bigger problem than snooping on them with read receipts. If you do have this problem, use the direct approach. Ask your boss talk to their boss.

Templates for recurring emails

The following message templates are the ones I use most frequently. Depending on your email application, you may be able to keep text for recurring emails in a draft folder. You can copy and paste text from the drafts for new messages. You should customize the templates for your own needs. The value of the templates is they give you quick options for recurring emails.

Template: Poor Subject

Be cautious with this template. I have learned the hard way that you can't use this template every time you receive a poor subject. It is totally inappropriate for senior members of your organization. Neither does it work for people that are junior to you, but in a different chain of command, unless you know them really well. They may complain to their boss that you are damaging their self-esteem. While you intend the message as a suggestion for improvement, they may interpret it more harshly (i.e., criticism). Customize it with humor or a light tone that suits your style and relationship with the recipient. Instead of writing "ugly" in the subject, you could substitute something like "icky" to convey more humor.

Subject: (ugly email subj)-[their original subject goes here]

BLUF: Please consider improving email subjects

Message Text: It would most helpful if you used clearer subjects. Like most people, I screen my email by subject. I like to know, from the subject alone, the action the sender wants. I don't mind being asked to do something, I just want to know when that happens so I can prioritize my work. Using really good subjects helps me identify actions and give you what you want faster. Creating really specific and useful email subjects is a skill you can improve over time.

[Paste "Tips for Writing Better Subjects" here]

Template: Ill-advised use of existing subject

Be cautious with this template too. The caveats for Poor Subject above apply to this template as well. Only use this with senders you know well.

Subject: (ugh, pls update)-[original subject goes here]

BLUF: Please consider updating the subject.

Introductory Text Option1: Please change the subject when the content of the message changes. I screen my email inbox by subject and using a subject that is not related to the content of the message just confuses me. It also might not motivate me to read your message as quickly as you want. Neither is a good thing. Creating really specific and useful email subjects is a skill you can improve over time. My aim for every email is to create a subject that makes the content clear from the subject alone.

or

Introductory Text Option2: Please note my modification to your subject. I screen my email inbox by subject and find that very specific, clear subjects really help me prioritize reading and responding to messages. This is true for others as well. Creating really specific and useful email subjects is a skill you can improve over time. My aim for every email is to create a subject that makes the content clear from the subject alone.

[After choosing one of the introductions, continue with this paragraph]

Tips for Writing Better Subjects

Creating a good email msg involves three steps:
   1. Understanding why you are writing and what you expect your reader to do
   2. Briefly stating what you need and when, and
   3. Finishing with a brief, descriptive subject. This is almost always different than what you used when you started composing. Your message content and purpose are the most clear after you write the

text. This is normal.

A descriptive subject instantly makes 1 and 2 clear. I typically read and re-read my subject line a few times before hitting send, asking "Will the recipient be able to quickly grasp the key information and action *from the subject line alone*?" Try to use no more than 30 characters to do this.

Bonus email tips:
  * assume that no one will ever read more than the first sentence of anything you write so make it count,
  * compose your message so the most important information fits on one screen,
  * summarize the content and reason for including every attachment,
  * invite people to meetings with meeting requests, not emails,
  * if you must use an email for a meeting invitation, put the topic/date/time/location in the subject and message body, NOT an attachment, and
  * get right to the point after your BLUF (Bottom Line Up Front) by explaining actions and importance before background information.

Template: What is a BLUF?

Note: I use this text to explain the concept of a BLUF (Bottom Line Up Front) and why it is so useful.

Subject: What is a BLUF?
or
Subject: What the BLUF? (funnier, but risky)
Message Text: BLUF is a term I learned in the Navy. It stands for "Bottom Line Up Front." It conveys the core idea of the message (the Bottom Line), including action, in just a few sentences at the top of an email (Up Front). It is the most efficient way to clearly state what the message is about (key issue) and what is expected (if anything) from readers. Using a BLUF is very efficient for communicating. It is more respectful of the recipient's time (no beating around the bush) and will be appreciated by your readers.
I hope you find this explanation helpful. I don't intend it to be abrupt, just compact and quick to read. If you have any questions, let

me know.

Template: Event Arranging

Subject: Need sked windows for [short event subject] [date range you are considering]

BLUF: I am trying to arrange a date and time for [event subject]. The purpose of the meeting [or call] is [one sentence description]. As soon as you can, please reply to all with your windows of availability, date and time, between [start date] and [end date]. When everyone has responded, I will propose a time and day for the [event] that is most suitable for everyone's calendar.

Template: Event Announcement

Note: Don't include the year in the announcement. It is almost never necessary and wastes valuable subject space. Abbreviate the topic title as much as possible to keep the total length of subject less than 30 characters. Include the location at the end of the subject.

Subject: [Call/Mtg/Training/etc.] [dd mmm time] [very brief topic] [location]

BLUF: [Brief description of topic] [call/mtg/training/etc.] will be [dd mmm time] in/at [location]. The purpose of the [event] is [brief purpose]. The [proposed] agenda is below [and more background information is included in the attachment] or A brief summary of the [presentation/training/demonstration] is below.
    Proposed Agenda -> note the responsible party for each item, if applicable
    * Introductions [person A]
    * Issue 1 [person B]
    * Issue 2 [person C]
    * Summary of Actions [meeting organizer]

Key points from Chapter 12

- The tools and templates in this chapter will jump start your communications effectiveness. They are based on the principles from this book and help you "just do it."

- The Email Ninja checklist collects all the key ideas of the PAASTUB system on one page. You can print the checklist and keep it near your computer as a guide.
- Subject keywords are the "tell" of your email, important cues at the start of the subject that telegraph the purpose. You can develop your own, but the list provided in this chapter will get you started.
- The email etiquette guide is a brief, clear description of dos and don'ts for sending better email. It is not a substitute for reading the book (of course), but is a succinct statement based on its principles that you can use to remind people of the most important parts.
- The templates for recurring email messages are for: providing subject guidance, explaining BLUFs, arranging events, and announcing events. They make it easier right away for you to send better email messages and help others improve. Keep them in your drafts folder so you can access them whenever you need them.

The next chapter shows how to apply the communications practices of an Email Ninja to text messaging.

Part 4 - Text Messaging

When will you finish
your project **??**

I don't know. I
keep getting
text messages.

Chapter 13 Guide to Text Messaging

BLUF: Most of the principles of this book apply to text messages as well as email. Texting almost always represents an interruption so stick to non-emotional issues, keep your messages brief and focused, and go light on slang and abbreviations. Try to be responsive to texts, but don't thoughtlessly give away your time and focus.

Introduction

If email is like sending a letter, texting is like poking someone next to you and handing them a note. Like poking someone in the physical world, texts can interrupt recipients for important, quick, timely communications. Just like poking someone repeatedly when they need to focus on something else, interruptions like text messages can be very irritating. Skillfully navigating the fine line between texts that are useful and annoying is what this chapter is about.

This chapter provides guidelines for focusing on the reader when you send text messages. The chapter has nothing about texting while driving, walking, or drunk. If you do those things, you need more help than a book like this can give you. This chapter is also not a universal guide to texting. I don't think such a thing is possible because the customs and norms for texting are constantly changing. What is normal and appropriate for text message communications varies widely by age, constantly evolving social customs, and social context (business, school, recreation).

Overview of Text Messaging

You can find lots of guides to text messaging etiquette on the internet. This chapter is a distillation of the most common ideas from the perspective of an Email Ninja. Focusing on the reader is still the fundamental principle.

Text messages can be very useful to communicate important information that is easily understood without having to take the extra time that a phone conversation typically involves. Phone calls are great ways to maintain social relations, communicate complex issues with some nuance, and convey emotions, but do you really need to bother someone in the midst of dinner preparations to tell them you are running late or to ask what kind of wine to bring? Subject to the guidelines below, perhaps not.

I consider the central feature of text messaging to be interruption, the ability to tap or poke someone to get their attention. The extent of the interruption depends on how the user has configured their text message notifications, which you can't control. However, one of the most important social norms in the physical world is *not* to interrupt people without good cause. Parents spend a lot of time teaching their children not to interrupt or distract them when they are talking to other people, conducting business on the telephone, putting things in a blender, out on a date, watching a movie or favorite television program, or concentrating on something difficult. Children or newcomers to an organization are usually taught, directly or indirectly, to observe what people are doing before blurting out what seems really important to them. Speakers are expected to assess the priority of their information relative to the ongoing situation. The simple rule I gave my sons when they were younger was, "If you are not spurting blood or the house is not on fire, what you have to say can wait." Adults that didn't learn this when they were growing up are just a pain to be around.

Interruptions are a pain because they require you to stop what you were doing or the conversation you were having, attend to the interruption, and then attempt to resume the previous activity without losing your mental "place." Despite the ubiquity of smart phones and wearable technology, both of which are actually designed to interrupt their users, skillful multitasking is myth (Burak, 2012). What the brain can do is rapidly switch from one task to another and this has consequences for performance on complex tasks or creative work

(Kraushaar and Novak, 2010; Ophira, Nass, and Wagner, 2009; Rubenstein, Meyer, and Evans, 2001). The brain is not capable of attending to more than one thing at a time and it is hard to remember where you left off when you get interrupted. You may be special and believe that the findings of numerous studies don't pertain to you. Dream on.

Even if you have attention super powers and suffer no loss of attention or effectiveness from interruptions, this doesn't apply to everyone else. The value a person places on their attention and focus depends on many factors. Since it is not easy for you to know what those factors are in advance, it is wise to send text messages with some caution.

The Important Things for Good Text Messages

The list that follows describes the most important things an Email Ninja considers when texting.

Keep it simple. Text messaging is not an efficient way to communicate complex issues, bad news, emotionally charged content, or make plans. I occasionally get lured into making plans via text from others and it almost never works. Call or email instead.

Don't text sensitive information. Don't send potentially upsetting news (like breaking up with someone) via text. This is best conveyed face-to-face or on the telephone. Letting family members know that another family member is in the hospital is fine, but provide all updates via email.

Text Awareness. Does the intended recipient know what a text message is? There is no point in texting someone that has no idea how to read and reply to them. While the number of people under the age of 60 that are ignorant of text messaging continues to shrink, such people do exist. The only way to know for sure is to ask them. If you think you are going to teach them, think carefully about the genie you are about to let out of the lamp. If you have any concerns about someone interrupting you or people close to you throughout the day (and night) with trivial messages, it might be best to let them remain ignorant of text messaging.

Get permission. Some people don't like to text or do so sparingly because they don't like the interruption it entails. In business contexts, it is best to ask if it is okay to text someone before you do it.

Know their app. One of the tricky things about texting is that everyone seems to have a favorite app for it. Many people are responsive to texts via that one app and only that app. You could find yourself texting someone all day without getting a response because you are not using someone's preferred app. People are seldom explicit about their preference so the best ways to learn which app they favor is a) ask them when you get their permission to send texts or b) use the app they use to send texts to you.

Identify yourself. This is a version of "don't send puzzles." Unlike email that always includes your name with the message, many texts are transmitted with just your phone number. If the recipient does not have an entry for you in their contacts list with that number, the phone number is the only thing they will see besides your message, which can be very confusing. They will have to figure out who you are from the context of the message. If you have any doubt, identify yourself briefly at the *beginning* of the text message. Something like "Fm Ralph S-" or "Ralph Soule here" is sufficient. None of this applies if you text with an app that registers its users like What's App, Facebook, or Viber.

Keep it short. Text messages are for quick thoughts and responses, not long descriptions of your day or extended monologues that are better placed in emails or letters. Three brief sentences is a good thumb rule for the longest text you should send. Anything longer belongs in email. Think of texts as preludes or follow-ups to a conversation, not the conversation itself. Don't waste time and space with filler text like "umm" or "y'all." This filler words have a place in face-to-face communication. In texts, they make the reading tedious.

Don't obsess about content. This is a corollary to "keep it short." Don't overthink your text message content. If you are going to be late, just text that with an estimate of your arrival time. You can worry later about whether this makes you look inconsiderate. Don't bother correcting most typos. The auto correct feature of most phones can create spectacular errors, but most recipients can overcome simple typos. If you do correct something, just resend with a single corrected word. Readers can figure this out too. Don't worry too much about punctuation. There are long blog posts devoted to the topic of whether ending your text message with a period can make you appear insincere to others. If this is something you worry about, you are overthinking text messaging.

No conversations. If you are over the age of twelve, texts are not for extended conversations. If you find yourself texting more than four messages to someone in rapid succession, pick up the phone or text "can you take a call now?" before you keep blathering on. In my case, I send a text "have to go now" when someone wants to converse via text. I have better things to do.

Be responsive. Responsiveness is just as important for text as it is for email, within limits. This is another important social norm. If you can tolerate a brief interruption to what you are doing, reply quickly to texts, just don't get carried away. When someone is just sending me information, I typically I respond with just "k" (short for "okay"), thx (short for "thanks"), or "rog" (short for "roger").

Block the unresponsive. Texting is just another form of social relations. Some people don't seem to grasp the importance of reciprocity in text messaging or any other form of social relations. They text you when they want something, but are totally unresponsive when you ask them for something (like paying back a loan). You are not going to change their attitudes or behaviors, but you can block them from texting you in the future. If you did loan them money, they are not likely to pay you back anyway. When they complain that you have not responded to a text (and they will), your reply could be "I don't check my texts very often."

Responsiveness costs. Your attention is an extremely scarce resource. Skilled multi-tasking is like unicorns, a myth. Sometimes it is better to disable text notifications on your smart phone, turn its screen face down, or put it in a drawer so you can get work done.

Don't nag. This is could be called "The Two Text Rule." If you text someone a few times and they don't respond, they probably are not going to so stop texting them, permanently. They either don't want to communicate with you, don't understand how to text, or are too disorganized or rude for you to expect responses. Don't waste your time on more texts to them.

Reply to ignored calls. Sometimes you cannot take a call. I think there is nothing wrong with sending a short text to the caller, although others may disagree. Some phones come with a variety of built-in replies for this situation to automate the process.

Don't reply to group texts. Sometimes you will receive texts that were sent to a group. While it is easy to reply with gushing comments about someone's pet ferret picture, *don't. Not even once.* Replying to a group text is the same as "reply to all" in email. Gush all you want in a separate text to the sender that leaves everyone else off distribution.

Be careful with slang. Texting slang or abbreviations requires caution. It is really easy to be misunderstood or convey the impression you are a thoughtless idiot. One example: sending LOL to someone attending a funeral because you thought it meant "Lots of Love" and they think it means "Laughing out Loud." I confused my son once by replying to a question with just one letter, "Y," which meant "yes" to me and "why?" to him. Opinions diverge about whether it is acceptable to use abbreviations like "u" for "you" and "u r" for "you are." One view is that super informal abbreviations are perfectly acceptable in texts. Another view is that using them makes you look like an uneducated clod. Just remember that while you get to choose how to type your messages, other people get to choose how to interpret them. Idiocy is in the eye of the beholder.

Sometimes a call is better than texting. For some last-minute communications, it is better to call than text, but this can be tricky. If you are not sure someone reads their text messages, sending a text at the last minute about running late for a meeting could be a waste of time. Call them instead. Unless you know someone is super-responsive to texts, don't text with urgent or emergency information.

Ignore misaddressed texts. Don't waste your time correcting someone you don't know for sending you texts in error, unless they keep sending you ferret pictures. If you think you need to inform senders they have the wrong number for their texts, the quick way to do it is reply with "wrong number." That should be a sufficient to motivate the sender to update their contacts. Otherwise, just ignore the ferrets and stay focused on the work you have to do.

A final note about text messaging etiquette that does not quite fit into the list. When you are face to face with others or operating heavy machinery, your eyes and attention should be on the people you are with and the things you are doing, not your phone. If you are expecting a text message from the Pope, the most polite thing to do is tell the people you are with and step out of the room to reply. Do not operate machinery while constantly glancing at your phone. While it may not initiate total protonic reversal, it would still be bad.

Key Points from Chapter 13

Text messaging shares some common features with email. Both can be used to communicate useful and sometimes important information to get work done and coordinate activities. Both can be quick to compose and send. Both can also be voracious consumers of time and focus needed to perform your best work. Both can be lengthy tangles of tangled, undisciplined thinking. Finally both can be great tools for getting things done at the keyboard of an Email Ninja.

Unlike email, which drops into a user's inbox and sits there until they process it, text messages are a poke in the ribs, designed to interrupt the recipient to focus on something else right now. An Email Ninja sets a very high bar for sending texts. As in real life, they only poke someone with a message when what they have to say is probably more important than *anything else the recipients have going on*. Otherwise, they send an email. Email Ninja's stay true to the most important principle of electronic communications: focus on the reader. They don't send texts just because it is easier for *them*.

- Unless you have super powers (if you aren't from another planet or a mutant, you **don't**), you don't multitask any better than anyone else. If you let yourself be interrupted anytime someone texts you, this is a decision to divert scarce attention from doing your best work.
- Texting is not an efficient way to make plans. You will spend far less time planning and discussing options on a phone call.
- Don't send bad or potentially upsetting news via text.
- Before you send a lot of texts to someone, ask them if they like to communicate this way and what their preferred app is.
- Identify yourself the first few times you text someone or if you haven't texted them in a long time. They might not recognize your number.
- Text messages should be brief, two or three sentences at most, but don't overthink or overcorrect spelling and punctuation.
- Don't bother correcting simple typos. Most readers will know what you meant.
- Don't have long conversations with text. Anything longer than four belongs in an email or on the phone. At four text messages, you are very close to breaching the text-phone/email efficiency threshold.
- Texts only take the amount of attention you give them. Respond quickly when possible, but ignore misaddressed texts, stop texting people that are seem unresponsive, and don't ignore people at the dinner table unless the Pope texts you.
- Don't keep texting people that don't reply consistently. You have better things to do.

- When you need to get work done, turn off text notifications or put your phone where you can't see or hear it.
- Use automated texts when you need to ignore a call, but don't forget to call back.
- Don't reply to group texts. Send a new text only to the original sender. If you can block other replies, do so or you will be interrupted many, many times.
- Be careful with slang and abbreviations in texts. Meaning changes of various terms are frequent and fluid. The line between being perceived as hip or an ignoramus can be very thin.
- Many times, calling someone is better than texting for urgent information. If they can't take the call, leave a message, send a text, or send a short email. Choosing an option depends on the other person's communications preferences, not yours.

This concludes Part 4. The next chapter is the last one of the book. It summarizes the ideas of the prior chapters and connects them to the underlying principles. The chapter finishes with a path to follow for changing your email practices and habits to communicate with more effectively.

Part 5 - Final Thoughts and Getting Started

How did you become
an Email Ninja?

Reading
Ralph's book,
then one step
at a time.

Chapter 14: Final Thoughts

BLUF: The ideas in this book reflect a system for communicating more effectively. You become an Email Ninja with a dual focus on your purpose and what the reader needs to accomplish it. The system in this book will increase the value in your communications.

Introduction

In this book, I have described a system of practices, strategies, and tools for electronic communication. Using them will help you accomplish your goals faster with more consistency. This chapter lists the main ideas of the prior chapters, the steps and the principles behind those ideas, and provides subject, BLUF, and final review checklists . It finishes with final thoughts on what you need to do to Become an Email Ninja.

Main Ideas from Seven Steps for Brilliant Email

1. This book describes a system of practices, strategies, and tools that improve your ability to communicate.

2. The seven steps for constructing effective emails help you create emails with action that is easy to spot, message text that is easy to read, and content that won't get you in trouble.

3. (**Purpose** Clear) The first step in making your purpose clear to readers is being clear yourself on why you are sending an email.

4. (**Action**-What and When) For emails requesting action, state what you need and when you need it right after the BLUF (Bottom Line Up Front).

5. (**Addressees**) Only send email to addressees that will change what they do based on the content.

6. (**Subject** as Art) Use the subject of your email to focus attention in a compelling way.

7. (Take Out the **Trash**) Remove everything that adds no value from email replies or forwards.

8. (**Ugly** Remarks Edited) Delete or paraphrase ugly (insensitive or intemperate) remarks in email to avoid pain and embarrassment.

9. (**BLUF**-ing) The Bottom Line Up Front (BLUF) of the message conveys the core ideas in three, plus or minus one, sentences.

10. (Email Strategies) The email strategies of this book are broad approaches applicable across all of your emails that promote greater effectiveness.

11. (Email Tactics) The email tactics of this book are high-leverage practices that improve productivity and effectiveness inside your messages.

12. (Email Ninja Tools) The tools and templates in chapter 12 make it easy to begin your journey to Become an Email Ninja.

13. (Text Messaging) Texting is all about interruption and brevity of message.

PAASTUB Steps and Their Principles *(Chapter 2)*

Step 1: Purpose is Clear: a clear purpose (desired outcome) is necessary for effective email

Step 2: Action: make it easy for readers see what you want by when

Step 3: Addressees: keep the right people informed

Step 4: Subject as Art: make the message content clear from the subject alone, using humor, irony and creative punctuation to make opening it compelling

Step 5: Take Out the Trash: remove all unnecessary text from email to make messages easy to scan

Step 6: Ugly Remarks Edited: keep yourself and others out of trouble by removing angry or rash text

Step 7: BLUF-ing: focus attention with a short message summary at the beginning of each message

Composing subjects-don't be a PIKER *(Chapter 6)*

Step 1 - Preliminary subject. Start composing the subject with your purpose clearly in mind. WILL THE PURPOSE OF THE EMAIL BE CLEAR FROM THE SUBJECT ALONE? Add a keyword, if you can, but don't get stuck on this step. Move quickly to the next step.

Step 2 - Inscribe (write) your message. Begin writing the message text. Get right to the point and try not to ramble with too much context. Your purpose will become clearer as you write. This is normal. Be clear about the action (what you want and when) right after the BLUF.

Step 3 - Keyword review. Return to the subject. Choose a keyword that best describes your message purpose or revise the one you chose in Step 1. Keywords aren't essential, but thinking about using one in this step gives you another opportunity to consider the best way to use the subject to get attention.

Step 4 - Edit the subject (again). You have written the message text so your purpose is clearer than when you started. Now your goal is to reduce the subject to **30 characters or less**. Use creative punctuation.

Step 5 - Re-read the subject at least once (slowly). Be sure it conveys the message text's **key idea**. Humor or irony make the email even more compelling.

Composing a BLUF (Chapter 9)

The BLUF needs to answer these questions, in this order, as succinctly as possible:

1. What is this about (the issue)?
2. What is the action (by whom and when)?
3. Why is this important?

If you need more than four sentence to explain the BLUF, you aren't being brief enough. Try reading it to a colleague to see what they think.

Final Email Review Checklist (Chapter 11)

- The subject keyword "spills the beans" of your message, including due dates for actions
- The subject length is about 30 characters and uses irony or humor, when possible, to get attention
- The action is the first part of the subject
- The BLUF states: what is the issue, what is the action, and why your message is important
- If the message is forwarded, the BLUF states why and what is expected from recipients
- The list of actions follows immediately after the BLUF
- Action due dates are in the subject and BLUF
- Background material follows the list of actions
- All attachments are summarized

- Anyone mentioned in the message text, or an organizational representative, is included as an addressee
- Other addressees are only the people that will change their behavior or plans based on the message content

Getting Started

All of the steps, strategies, and tools in this book are important. Each is a key element of a systematic approach to email that will make you a much better communicator. They are like gears in a precision machine, each supporting the other as part of an overall design for better communications. Just don't let the number of gears overwhelm you.

No one becomes a Ninja overnight or by changing just one thing. Adopting the system and its laser focus on readers is not hard. You can start incorporating key elements into the way you compose and address email messages a step at a time. All great journeys begin with just a few steps. Below are concrete steps to get you started on your journey. You can Become an Email Ninja one step at a time.

- Turn off automatic "reply to all." RIGHT NOW. This won't change your email composition skills, but it is a big step toward focusing on the right readers. It is also an easy action to take. There are very few circumstances when everyone on a group email needs to know why you can't attend a meeting.
- Print a copy of the PAASTUB and PIKER checklists and keep them by your computer to review as you write new emails. Another good step is to write these checklists on small index cards. There is research that suggests writing notes by hand helps you remember them better (Mueller & Oppenheimer, 2014). You can use cards of different colors so you can tell them apart easier, they stand out better, and are more likely to attract your attention when composing email.
- After the subject (not "meeting"), begin the first sentence of every email with "My desired outcome is:" and finish that thought in no more than two sentences. Really. For example, "My purpose is to inform my boss that I need his help on my project." The best way to make your purpose clear to yourself is to write what it is, at least what you think it is, when you start composing. The purpose will likely evolve as you compose your email, which is something you should expect.

Clarity of purpose is like flavor in cooking: it develops over time from the ingredients you add. You can replace the "My desired outcome is" text with the BLUF before you send the email message.

- Start creating better subjects, using keywords like "info" and "action." Explain what you are doing the first few times. "I am changing the way I write subjects. I hope you find it useful." Change the subject on replies when it no longer applies or is just plain bad ("meeting"). Use your PIKER checklist card to help. Add some humor when you can. Brief, clear, and sometimes humorous email subjects are like attention magnets in a recipient's inbox.

- Print the three parts of a BLUF (what the email is about, what action is necessary, and why the email is important) or write them on a card too. Keep the list by your computer next to the PAASTUB and PIKER checklists. Use a three, plus or minus one, sentence BLUF for every email longer than one paragraph. Explain what a BLUF is for the people that need it.

- Explain the reason for every email you forward or when you add someone new. Change the subject if you can do better than the original sender. Edit the text (Step 5: Take Out the Trash) of all forwarded emails to remove all unnecessary text, especially "dear [anyone]," "Hi," and repeated signatures.

- Adopt the strategies in chapter 10, just one or just a few at a time. Improve your skill at using them before adopting more.

- Begin practicing the tactics in chapter 11, one category of email at a time.

- Print or write the final review checklist on another index card and use it when you send email. Think deliberately about each step so you don't rush through the review. That would defeat the purpose. Make sure you have good alignment between the email contents, the subject, and the BLUF.

- Discuss with your team the value of adopting the email etiquette guide. Customize the draft to suit your team's needs.

- Copy the templates for recurring emails to your drafts folder. Customize them to reflect *your* style. Use them to coach, not berate, people that send you a lot of email. Help them improve what they send to you. Be gentle when you explain an opportunity to improve so it does not come across too harshly.

At this point, you know every part of my email system for more effective communications. I hope you are enthusiastic about becoming an Email Ninja, a person who focuses on readers to design highly effective emails to accomplish their goals. Using the behaviors and strategies in this book starts your virtuous learning cycle for more effective communications. The behaviors and strategies will improve your ability to communicate with others and get the results that are most important to you and your organization. You will be able to extend the cycle of more effective communications by teaching others.

Caution

A few words of caution about using the email system described in this book. Now that you know the system, you can begin your journey to improve how you communicate by email. Based on my experience in the chaotic and fast-paced business world, the email practices, strategies, and tools in the book work really well. Appropriately applied, they will surely improve your ability to get what you need to accomplish your goals. You will find that using them changes the way you think and communicate about your priorities.

My caution is this: be gentle with others that have not read the book. As you use the practices and adapt them to your needs, go easy on your less enlightened colleagues and subordinates. Be skillful, patient, and a good teacher, not an evangelist. While I would personally love it if you would just buy the book for as many of your colleagues as possible, that probably won't be sufficient or particularly helpful to achieve lasting change.

Based on extensive experience, my suggestion is that you guide other people to better email practices gently and patiently. Frame any feedback you provide to people about their emails in the form of "this is the help I need to be productive" and not as "you worthless piece of excrement." Adults don't respond well to the latter. Nor do they appreciate it when someone tells them how they should think and behave. If your feedback is in the form of what **you need** to **help them**, the feedback is more about you than them. This goes down a lot better than a frontal assault on their email practices.

Some of your more reflective colleagues will notice that your emails are different and may start using much better subjects based on your example alone. I have seen this many times and it is very satisfying. I always congratulate people when I see really good subjects ("very nice subject").

Explain what a BLUF is the first time you include one. I noted that in the list above, but it is worth repeating. With the "What is a BLUF" template in your Drafts folder, it only takes seconds to explain what it is and why you used it (just below the BLUF works well). Be specific about how you think it helps *them*.

Tell people about my email system and why you use it in casual conversation, *when they ask about it*. If the people you work with want to know more about the system, *then* you can point them to my book and buy them a copy. The "pull" approach to skills improvement works much better than pushing.

Good luck in your personal journey to make electronic communications better, one email at a time. Writing this book was my part. The rest is up to you.

References

Allen D. (2015). Getting things done: The art of stress-free productivity. London: Penguin Books.

Burak, L. (2012). Multitasking in the University Classroom. *International Journal for the Scholarship of Teaching and Learning* Article 8, 6(2). Available at: https://doi.org/10.20429/ijsotl.2012.060208

Drucker, P.F. (1999). Management: tasks, responsibilities, practices. London: Taylor & Francis).

Etiquette. (2016). In Cambridge Academic Content Dictionary. Retrieved from http://dictionary.cambridge.org/us/dictionary/english/etiquette.

Gibson, J. J. (1977). The theory of affordances. In R. E. Shaw & J. Bransford (Eds.), Perceiving, Acting, and Knowing. Hillsdale, NJ: Lawrence Erlbaum Associates.

Gibson, J. J. (1979). The ecological approach to visual perception. Boston: Houghton Mifflin.

Haidt, J. (2012). The righteous mind: Why good people are divided by politics and religion. New York: Random House.

Heath, C., & Heath, D. (2011). Switch. New York: Random House.

Kraushaar, J.M., & and Novak, D.C. (2010). Examining the affect (sic) of student multitasking with laptops during lecture. Journal of Information Systems Education, 21(2). 241-251.

Miller, C. A. (2002). Definitions and dimensions of etiquette. In *Proc. AAAI Fall Symposium on Etiquette and Human-Computer Work.* Palo Alto, CA: Association for the Advancement of Artificial Intelligence.

Mueller, P. A., & Oppenheimer, D. M. (2014). The pen is mightier than the keyboard: Advantages of longhand over laptop note taking. *Psychological Science,* 25(6), 1159-1168.

Norman, D. A. (1999). Affordance, conventions, and design. Interactions, 6(3), 38-43.

Ophira, Nass, and Wagner's (2009). Cognitive control in media multitaskers. *PNAS Proceedings of the National Academy of Sciences of the United States of America,* 106, 15583–15587. doi: 10.1073/pnas.0903620106

Rubinstein, J. S., Meyer, D. E., & Evans, J. E. (2001). Executive Control of Cognitive Processes in Task Switching. *Journal of Experimental Psychology: Human Perception and Performance,* 27(4), 763-797. doi: 10.1037/0096-1523.27.4.763

Afterword

How This Book Came to Be

A colleague and I wrote a voluntary email etiquette guide in 2005. We were being swamped by bad email practices in the organization and wanted to do something to make the problem slightly less bad. Prior to that, I taught people about email and communicating more effectively one on one for several years, but I lacked a comprehensive statement of all the important ideas. The email etiquette guide was a start. Later, I refined the ideas and strategies from the guide into a ten-page strategy document that went beyond etiquette to address tools and techniques for high-leverage communications. I updated that document many times and shared it widely. I still get asked for copies.

I started putting ideas together for this book in 2013 when I wondered if a) I had enough material for a book and b) I could actually write a book, any book. I put the project aside while I finished my doctoral studies and dissertation Human and Organizational Learning program at the George Washington University in 2016.

I am always collecting new ideas for communicating more effectively in email. If you have an idea that you think I should have included, send it to me at ralph.soule.book@icloud.com. If I update this book and can use your idea, I will add it and give you credit.

About the Author

Dr. Ralph Soule served in the U.S. Navy for 29 years, retiring as a Captain in 2011. He has extensive experience in the operation, testing, maintenance, and repair of nuclear-powered aircraft carriers and submarines. He was assigned to multiple Navy staffs, ships, and shore commands. Several of these organizations had thousands of employees. He wrote email etiquette guides and policies for several organizations because the email practices were driving him crazy. He has provided training on his system for better email communications to small and large groups and mentored many people, one tip at a time. He received his doctorate in Human and Organizational Learning from the George Washington University in 2016. He lives with his wife in Albuquerque, New Mexico, which is the only one of the United States that has "USA" on some of its license plates. Some people apparently get confused about that.